Angela Remembered

Angela Remembered

The life of Angela Gradwell Tuckett
by Rosie MacGregor

www.watermarx.co.uk

Published by WaterMarx
on behalf of White Horse (Wiltshire) Trades Council.

Published in 2015 by WaterMarx
The Grain Store, High Street, Urchfont
Devizes, Wiltshire SN10 4QH
on behalf of White Horse (Wiltshire) Trades Council.
Cover design by Bob Naylor, WaterMarx
Cover Picture of Angela Gradwell at the gates of Greenham
Common by Bob Naylor: Report Digital

ISBN 978-0-9570726-3-3

Printed by Sarum Colourview
Unit 8, Woodford Centre
Lysander Way, Old Sarum, Salisbury SP4 6BU
01722 343 600
www.sarumcolourview.co.uk

Disclaimer
Views expressed in this publication are those of the author and
not necessarily those of WaterMarx or White Horse (Wiltshire)
Trades Council.

Ted and Ivy Poole.
Picture by Bob Naylor: WaterMarx

To Ted and Ivy Poole
Great friends and good
comrades who shared their
politics and love of folk music
with Angela, and who helped
inspire my decision to write
this book.
I hope they enjoy reading it.

About the author

Rosie MacGregor, born in Chesterfield and brought up in Matlock, Derbyshire now lives near Bath. The late Phillip Whitehead, writer, television producer and Labour MP for Derby North, inspired her to take an interest in socialism and left wing politics.

She moved to the West Country after leaving school and is a graduate of the University of the West of England, working in architecture and town planning in the private sector and local government.

Rosie MacGregor
Picture by Bob Naylor: WaterMarx

She has at various times been a member of NALGO, now UNISON, the Musicians Union and National Union of Journalists.

As well as her full time job she spent 25 years writing about folk, roots and world music for Bath Chronicle and for a variety of different music publications under the name Rosie Upton for which she is also well known as a folk singer.

She has been active in the union for most of her working life holding various positions including South West Regional Convenor for UNISON during which time she spoke on a variety of public service issues on numerous platforms including the Trades Union Congress. She is currently Chair of South West Regional TUC, Chair of Chippenham Constituency Labour Party and Secretary of White Horse (Wiltshire) TUC and continues to represent UNISON on various committees.

Contents

Introduction

I was first aware of Angela when I was a student in Bristol in the early 1970s when she must have been in her late sixties, though to me, a first year student, she appeared much older. Even so she was a commanding figure, tall and angular with a strong face, neat grey hair, had it not been for a few fly-away wisps, and a smart if somewhat peculiar dress sense. Only later did I learn of her astonishing story and like many others I became very fond of her and admired her greatly.

My initial meeting with her was on my first of many visits to Bristol's Folk Tradition held, at that time, upstairs in the Old Duke in Old King Street. During the evening Angela was invited to sing. Her performance was memorable, not so much for the pleasing delivery, but for its unabashed individuality and her authoritative presence. A high-pitched slightly strained voice accompanied by concertina was an acquired taste. She wrote many of her own songs and brought her own unique interpretation to English folk song.

Afterwards, back in someone's flat in Redland, I was keen to find out more about her and was told she was a retired solicitor. It figured, her speaking voice had the perfectly formed vowel sounds of the upper middle class. Some weeks later I discovered more about her and was startled to find out that someone who had appeared to me as a rather straitlaced, if slightly eccentric, older 'lady' had a history of militancy and radical politics.

Angela was a remarkable woman and her story inspirational. She excelled at sport, she was a scholar and historian who wrote songs, plays, poetry and books, she was a solicitor, journalist, political activist, feminist, peace campaigner, folk musician and trade unionist, and was a qualified air pilot. During her lifetime she met many of the great artists, musicians, writers, intellectuals and politicians of the day.

What is it that sets some people apart and motivates them to experience more than most and give so much to society? Whatever it is, Angela had it in abundance. She had energy, drive and intellect but was also resourceful and resolute. Her's was a life well lived, for the most part not selfishly, but fearlessly and responsibly, with a genuine belief in social justice and a determination to take action and follow through what she knew to be right.

She was a complex character and passionate about her beliefs. Never afraid to speak out or take action against oppression in its many forms, sometimes at considerable risk, or if she felt it necessary to raise awareness of injustice or inequality.

I hope, had Angela been alive to read this short biography, she would have considered it to be a worthy tribute to her many achievements, as would all those who knew her. It has not been an easy task unravelling the facts from the legend. I found many contradictions and inconsistencies in people's memories of events and recollections of what she had told them. Some stories had been embellished but others played down. Equally, many of those I spoke to had told me such incredible tales that I found them barely believable, only to subsequently discover that the events they described were indeed true. Often confirmed by records held by various institutions together with notes in Angela's own diaries. There was sometimes an element of truth even in some of the most unbelievable.

Occasionally I found Angela's own memoirs, written when she was already elderly and long after one particular event or another, to be confused in places. Memories are not always accurate, some are real but others may be imagined, our recall after a long time has elapsed is not always precise and even though the event itself can be remembered perfectly well the interpretation may be different. She described, for example, meeting a talented young artist who was drawing quick cartoon sketches at the opening of a play. Writing many years after the event she commented that he later 'found great fame' and that 'his name was Gerald Scarfe'. I have no doubt that she met a gifted young cartoonist but it wasn't Scarfe who was not born until many years after her supposed meeting with him.

This profile of Angela has required careful cross-referencing and piecing together to complete the jigsaw. Even so I could find no evidence for some of the stories I was told, such as the account from a number of different people that she had gone out to join the International Brigade and fight in Spain during the Spanish Civil War. Whilst she certainly travelled to Spain and had seen the effect of the bombing of Guernica, she was in USA for nearly two years during the civil war. She supported the Spanish Republic in its struggle but given the timeframe it is unlikely she took an active part other than visiting the country, raising awareness and in writing and distributing propaganda in UK and the USA. Stories can all too easily become exaggerated in the telling and re-telling. Where I could find no supporting evidence of a variety of improbable incidents I have not included them as part of this life story.

I never established how she preferred to be known and different people from the various groups who knew her referred to her by different names as she did when introducing herself. I knew her both as Angela Tuckett amongst her friends in Bristol and as Angela Gradwell in Swindon. Some called her Angela Tuckett Gradwell and others Angela Gradwell Tuckett. I have gone with the latter for no good reason other than that the names are in an alphabetical sequence.

–1–
Family, Friends
and
Early Years

There were two branches of the Tuckett family in the Bristol area. The Tucketts had moved from Looe in Cornwall in the 18th century and both branches were descended from James Tuckett of Looe, Angela's great, great, great grandfather. He had been married twice, both wives were sisters, and it was their descendants who in turn founded the two dynasties in the Bristol area. James' first wife was Anna Debell and their son Philip Debell Tuckett founded the Frenchay dynasty. Five years after Anna's death James married her younger sister Mary and it was their son John Debell Tuckett, Angela's great, great grandfather, who later moved to Bristol. It was perhaps the opportunities that the city could offer that encouraged this move and possibly also the family connection between the two half brothers that both should choose to relocate to Bristol. Also, the Tucketts were Quakers and in moving to a city where there were many Quaker families may have been seen as an opportunity to avoid discrimination and gain wealth, esteem and prosperity.

Certainly Looe by comparison with Bristol had its limitations. It was a small village on the south-eastern edge of the Cornish peninsular and dependent for the most part on the fishing and mining industries. Falmouth and Plymouth had increased significantly in size and popularity as ports and as a result, by the late 18th century, Looe's importance and prosperity was in decline, just about the time that the Tuckett brothers moved away. Bristol not only shared a maritime history and trading links with Cornwall but in the 18th century it was the second largest city in England after London and also the most profitable port, before Liverpool in the 19th century overtook its importance. A vast array of goods, both import and export, flooded through Bristol docks including tea, cane sugar, cocoa and tobacco on which much of the wealth of the city relied, but also regrettably the slave trade. The Merchant Venturers who were traders and entrepreneurs had controlled the port of Bristol since the 13th century and contributed to its pre-eminence, not simply as a trading port, but an embarkation point from which explorers set out to discover the world. However, by the 17th century these traders were actively involved in the slave trade and a number of Bristol Quaker families owned slave ships and were successful merchants, some even owning their own plantations.

There was an ethical dilemma for the Quakers and from the latter half of the 18th century they accepted that slavery was morally wrong and they went on to become leaders of the Abolitionist movement. I was relieved to find no evidence of any Tuckett involvement with slavery other than as abolitionists, or that they had joined The Merchant Venturers as the name Tuckett does not appear in its register of names. Indeed Philip Debell Tuckett, of the Frenchay family, was a prominent and outspoken abolitionist.

The Frenchay Tucketts were an eminent Bristolian Quaker family who lived at The Manor House in Frenchay and whose members included merchants, explorers, social reformers and philanthropists, famously Francis Fox Tuckett, a distinguished mountaineer, and Frederick Tuckett who founded Dunedin in New Zealand. The Tuckett family and another Quaker family, The Frys, came to dominate what was then the small village of Frenchay and their influence on the city of Bristol and beyond was massive both in terms of economic prosperity and in the welfare of its people. Angela's grandfather Coldstream Tuckett was a member of the second branch of the family who

Promotional provisions tin produced for A C Tuckett of Bristol (Grocer and Wine Merchant) circa 1900

Tuckett's Buildings at the junction of Stokes Croft with Cheltenham Rd and Ashley Rd

had settled within the city. He was a tea merchant who lived in Stokes Croft and ran a prosperous grocery business in what is still known as Tuckett's Buildings. It is an imposing group of three buildings dating from the late 19th century at the junction of Stokes Croft with Cheltenham Road and Ashley Road.

During the time that Angela's family were trading here it was an important area of the city with thriving industry and commerce adjoining what were then the prestigious and fashionable neighbourhoods of Montpelier, Kingsdown and St Pauls. Parts of these areas especially Stokes Croft and St Pauls suffered a massive decline in the 20th century but not until after the family had moved away.

Angela was proud of her Tuckett heritage and its Quaker origins, both on her father's side of the family but also the Frenchay branch. The families were not especially close but the Frenchay branch regularly referred to their 'Bristol cousins' as did those in Bristol of their counterparts. She was equally proud of her Cornish ancestry and assisted her father on several trips to Looe to discover the family history, though not always with the greatest success, but finding that there were still many Tucketts living in the Looe area.

3

If the spirit of adventure and freedom as well as a desire for peace and compassion can be inherited within family groups then these traits had been passed to Angela in no small measure.

Angela Mary Tuckett was born on 15 January 1906 into an affluent household at 5 Beaufort Buildings in Clifton, Bristol. It was a smart five-storey end of terrace Georgian house, just round the corner from the prestigious Clifton Mall and not far from the Suspension

No 5 Beaufort Buildings today

Bridge over the Avon Gorge. It was the largest house in the terrace with a dual frontage and the main reception rooms looked out over part of Clifton Down. Clifton at the time was the most prosperous area of the city with many fine examples of Georgian, Regency and Victorian architecture. Most of the properties in the area were in family occupation and all would have employed several servants. The census records reveal that Angela's family had a housekeeper Eliza Millard and a domestic servant Annie Sims. Massive changes swept through the city during and after the First World War and Angela would later on have seen at first hand during the 1920s and 30s these grand houses falling into disrepair and rented out in multiple occupation or being converted into flats. She would not have seen the regeneration of Clifton that happened towards the end of the 20th century and its return to being one of the most fashionable parts of Bristol, or the family home, once blackened with soot now restored to the colour of mellow Bath stone.

Her father Richard Clapson Tuckett was a local solicitor who founded a dynasty of Bristol based solicitors. Her mother Edna Mary Stacy, a singer and dancer who taught ballet and became choreographer for Bristol Amateur Operatic Society, was born in Weston-super-Mare, though her family subsequently moved to a large house in Cotham Road, Bristol as their father Henry's career progressed necessitating a move to Bristol.

Angela had two older siblings, a sister Phyllis Joan, always known as Joan, and a brother Coldstream. Sadly, Angela's mother died at the age of thirty-two when Angela was born but there was a large and loving family to nurture the child. An aunt from the Tuckett side of the family moved in soon after Angela's birth to look after the young family. Unlike the Tucketts, the Stacy family were not Quakers but Church of England. When Angela's father married Edna Stacy on 6 June 1894 it was in Christchurch on Clifton Down Road where the Stacy family worshipped. Although Richard had been born and brought up as a Quaker it would have been traditional for the wedding to be arranged by Edna's parents and for the marriage to take place in the bride's family church. When Angela was christened on 12 February 1906 it was at the high Anglo-Catholic All Saints' Church in Pembroke Road, Clifton. It is unclear whether Richard Clapson Tuckett remained a Quaker following his marriage to Edna or why Angela was christened, not at the church where her parents married, but at another nearby. Unusually both Angela's father and his brother Frank Coldstream Tuckett married into the Stacy family with Frank marrying Beatrix, known as Trixie, another of the Stacy sisters. It would be interesting to discover how these two families that were so different, or superficially so, came to be so closely interlinked. It would be revealing to learn how Richard Clapson Tuckett, a respectable young solicitor and grocer's son, met Edna Stacy and married into this fascinating left-wing family of original thinkers, feminists and artists. It is possible, given that a specific area of Richard's work was in defending civil liberties and community rights of access to common land, that they met through his work or that he shared their socialist principles. The latter is highly probable given his Quaker origins and beliefs. Though perhaps even in a city the size of Bristol there would have been plenty of opportunities for those with either money or influence, or who shared similar interests, to meet at a variety of social functions and other events.

Angela as a child on the left, her brother Coldstream and older sister Joan with their father

I was equally interested to discover the origins of the name Coldstream as a family name given that it is an extremely unusual first name. I assumed there would be no connection with the Coldstream Guards, given the Quaker origins of the family, and it seemed unlikely that there was any Scottish link either. However, I discovered that Philip Debell Tuckett, Angela's Great Grandfather, married Elinor Harris, whose parents were Francis Harris and Isabella Coldstream, hence the tradition of using Isabella's family name through several generations. Francis Harris was at the time a prosperous merchant and sugar refiner based at Lewins Mead, Bristol. The Harris family were also prominent non-Conformists who worshipped at the Baptist Chapel in Bristol's Broadmead. Francis's father was Alderman John Harris who, as a founding member of the Bristol committee for the abolition of slavery, attended its first meeting in 1788 and signed its petition to abolish this abhorrent trade.

No 5 Beaufort Buildings must have been a progressive and creative home where Angela was encouraged to think for herself and take an interest in the arts and politics. Certainly one of her mother's sisters, Enid, who died before Angela was born, was a well-known socialist and a campaigner for women's rights, a founding member of the Independent Labour Party and a member of the Gasworkers' Union who took part in the Bristol Cotton Workers Strike of 1890. She was known to be an exceptionally talented and persuasive speaker who inspired those who listened to her. Despite her early death at only 35 years in 1903, Enid's achievements were to be an inspiration to the young Angela and her sister Joan. Angela's grandparents on her mother's side were Rose (Rosina) Deeley and Henry Stacy, an artist, who had three daughters, Enid, Beatrix and Edna and two sons Paul and Charles. Henry was a founding member of The School of Art in Weston-super-Mare and subsequently taught art at Bristol University and had a studio at his house in Cotham. Later, he moved to Willsbridge between Bath and Bristol. He was a leading member of a group of artists known as The Bristol Savages and knew many of the artists and intellectuals of the day, including his friend William Morris, who were regular visitors to his studio. He is known to have painted a trade union banner for the Gasworkers' Union at his daughter Enid's request and this is still in existence today in the archives of Blaise Castle Museum though it was on loan and displayed in an exhibition about William Morris in The National Portrait Gallery in the autumn of 2014, whilst this book was being written.

Angela, in the foreword to one of her song-books 'Sing and Stay Human', wrote: "These are songs meant for singing with people – not at them. The earliest wrote itself in 1919, the latest in the nineteen eighties. But, in a way, they started very much earlier, as my granddad, Henry Stacy, would understand.

The Gasworkers Union banner

"There was always such fun in his Bristol studio – everybody singing, dancing, saying poems, making up plays and operas. Not only the family, but all the Socialist Society's visiting speakers and friends:

Edward Carpenter, Bernard Shaw, William Morris, Peter Curran and Eleanor Marx, as well as Charles Marson, with the folk-songs from his Parish in Somerset. And always, all the generations of kiddies down the years. Even me. I remember being the Little Match Girl in the opera-ballet we invented in the garden at Willsbridge when Uncle Charlie came home from Australia in the summer of 1914. Then, with a pointer twice my size, I was the one to display the singing tableaux, about Kaiser Wilhelm playing with matches, in the church hall that first wartime Christmas.

"Old and young, all had their part to play and make that harmony we all longed for. As now."

Her life seems almost to have been mapped out from childhood when, as she told a friend, one of her earliest memories was taking Mrs (Emmeline) Pankhurst's hand, dragging her by the arm across a room to a chair and sitting on her knee! It could so easily have been a life of privilege but instead she chose to fight for the rights of others. Family friend Charles Marson, vicar of Hambridge and both a founder of the Christian Socialist Society and member of the Fabian Society, was a friend of Cecil Sharp. This must surely have been influential in her love of folk music even though she was only 8 years old when he died. Marson's wife Chloe was a Suffragist and friend of Philippa Fawsett (Millicent Fawsett's daughter) and the knowledge that they were not only family friends but campaigning for women's rights also influenced a young Angela.

The eminent British sculptor Doris Kathleen Flinn had lived at the house in 5 Beaufort Buildings for four years from 1923, and her plaster plaque of Angela's sister entitled 'Portrait Head of Joan Tuckett' made in 1925 is in Bristol Museum and Art Gallery.

Her studio was located close by in the centre of Clifton at Boyce's Avenue. She also made a sculpture of Angela's father entitled 'RC Tuckett Esq' and one of Angela entitled 'Lawyer, Athlete, Aviator, Woman, 1935' but current whereabouts, even if they still exist, are not known. Doris Flynn and Joan Tuckett later shared a home at The Rookery, East Dundry near Bristol to which Angela was a regular visitor until her sister's early death. Throughout her life Angela loved the visual arts and more especially the Arts and Crafts Movement led by William Morris who was much influenced by John Ruskin and shared his socialist principles. Although he had died before her birth, Morris had been a close friend of her grandfather. Angela later became a member of the William Morris Society and sat on its Editorial Committee.

Angela Remembered

–2–
Growing Up,
Love and Moving On

Angela attended Clifton High School, a private girl's school on College Road that was a short walk from her home. It was a progressive non-denominational school that did not discriminate on the basis of social class and was open to any girl of good character. She excelled in this environment, not just academically but at sport, especially hockey in which she out-shone her contemporaries, and was a member of the school's 1st XI. Her teachers expected her to go to Oxford, but Angela had other ideas. She considered becoming a Physical Training Teacher but left school aged 16 in the autumn of 1922 despite her teachers urging her to remain. Clifton High School today in its relatively short list of 'Remarkable Alumni' credits Angela Tuckett as one of its 'Unsung Heroines' — 'The first qualified female solicitor to work in Bristol'.

Clifton High School as is today

Angela centre row 5th from left with Clifton High School 1st XI hockey team circa 1922

The role of women in society was beginning to change in the 1920s. Although women had taken on men's jobs during the First World War they were expected, after hostilities had ended, to return to their roles as domestic servants, housewives and mothers. However, women were becoming better educated since the school leaving age had increased to fourteen in 1918 and all women had gained the right to vote in 1920. Many were simply not satisfied to return to their pre-war status after the war and this was especially so for well-educated middle class women. Even so, the majority of women remained in their traditional roles but extraordinarily for a woman in the first part of the 20th century, Angela studied law and qualified as the first female solicitor in Bristol. Women were not allowed to practice law until 1919, when the Sex Disqualification (Removal) Act was passed, and in 1922 the first women successfully completed their legal examinations and were subsequently, on completion of their articles, allowed to become solicitors. So on her seventeenth birthday in 1922, Angela was articled to her father's Bristol based legal practice at 26 Orchard Street in the centre of the city. She became the first female law student in Bristol in January 1923 and completed her law examinations as an external student of the University of London in 1928. She was enrolled as a solicitor on 14 January 1929 having passed her final examination for the Law Society on 23 November 1928. Once qualified she was placed in charge of her father's Weston-super-Mare office at 39 High Street; her sister Joan, although eleven years older, qualifying as a solicitor shortly afterwards. Their brother Coldstream also qualified as a solicitor and joined the family firm which subsequently moved to larger premises at 3 Unity Street. The name Tuckett remained until relatively recently associated with the legal practice founded by Angela's father in Bristol.

26 Orchard Street (with bicycle outside) looking towards 3 Unity Street

Angela states that she experienced few problems being a woman in a predominantly male profession but soon after qualifying found many women consulted her and sought her advice on various personal and matrimonial issues. Her father also had a strong social conscience and placed great emphasis and value on treating people fairly, no matter what their background, which seems to have typified the family. He had become an acknowledged authority on the laws relating to footpaths and common land, fighting many legal battles over the rights of access on behalf of his clients. As Honourable Secretary of the

South West of England Footpaths Preservation Society he frequently found himself in the position of defending Commoners' Rights through the courts and was instrumental in keeping Rodway Common, a large area of common land to the north of the city open for public enjoyment. I was told by Angela's step-daughter Judith Gradwell that there was one such case early in Angela's career that her father had handed over to her about a disputed Right of Way. It was the first case she had handled that required a court appearance and a barrister to present the case but she did not meet him until the day of the hearing. On meeting Angela he exclaimed 'My God, a woman, we've lost'! They won of course, apart from anything else Angela would have done thorough research, but it might have taught him a lesson about women's abilities and achievements. Angela would no doubt be shocked by the reality of how much still needs to be realised. However, her own achievements and contribution to paving the way for greater equality should not be diminished. She must have been extremely busy in her new role yet, perhaps because she needed an opportunity to meet and share experiences with other professional women who were still in a minority, she found time to join the Bristol Soroptimists. This had been the first society of its type to be founded in the UK as a 'Venture Club for Women' in 1920 specifically for professional and businesswomen. It had just amalgamated with the American Soroptimists in 1930 when Angela joined.

Both Tuckett sisters had taken an active interest in left-wing politics and this was to become even more proactive during the Great Depression. The plight of the unemployed in Bristol and the 1931 Welsh Hunger Marchers, as they came through the city, were to have a profound effect on them; and they joined the Communist Party of Great Britain, taking food and copies of the Daily Worker to the marchers each day.

Angela states in her autobiography that to join the Communist Party was 'unavoidable'. This determination had begun in 1929 when, whilst working in Weston-super-Mare, she had decided to drive over 80 miles straight from work to Malvern Festival to see the new Bernard Shaw play 'The Apple Cart'. 'It struck me so powerfully that I decided to return night after night, sleeping in the Malvern Hills in my Austin Seven each time. This twenty-three year old was spell-bound to watch how politics and the government of the country worked, no matter the party allegedly in power. It was striking to see what must face a then just coming in Labour Government and the threat of control of them by the civil service and the hierarchy generally.' In order to amuse Shaw she sent him a message after one performance that she was coming to see the play every night and sleeping in the hills in her car. That night he drove out into the Malverns just as she was 'bedding-down' to check if it was true!

A few days later she met her future husband John Gustave Pilley for the first time. He was seven years older than her, had served in the army in France during the First World War and was now a university lecturer. She had been playing tennis in Clifton with a friend. John and a university colleague were playing on the next court and invited them to join them for tea after the game. 'There was a torrent of discussion on current events and John declared at once that he must teach me Marxism. Here at last was somebody quite different from the two previous boyfriends with whom I had gone for long country walks, dances with a moderate degree of sexual relationship but no success in getting any discussion on the things which were becoming so important to me.'

It is clear that Angela, a passionate young woman looking for romance and adventure, was deeply smitten and they soon embarked on a physical relationship. John was a good-looking man and must have appeared sophisticated and worldly in comparison to her previous younger boyfriends. Photographs of Angela at this time confirm that she too was a strikingly beautiful young woman if not conventionally pretty; tall, slim, well dressed and elegant. Hardly surprising then that John and Angela were instantly attracted to each other. It is a very different portrait of Angela from photographs taken later in life when fashion was clearly not at the forefront of her thoughts and pretty dresses had been replaced first by smart suits, making her appear every bit the professional woman, and later still by weatherworn jackets emblazoned with badges and emblems in support of her political beliefs.

Meeting John Pilley widened her knowledge of life and politics but also resulted in what she later described as 'undergoing a nightmare backstreet abortion'. Abortion in the 1920s was a very risky business but for many desperate young girls and women there was no alternative. Contraception was not readily available and the methods or devices were unreliable. The social stigma of giving birth outside marriage drove many young girls to seek an abortion or to commit suicide, and for many married women faced with an unwanted

Angela as a young woman

pregnancy after many years of childbearing it was poverty that was another driving force. Many died as a result from the lack of hygiene and invasive methods by people with little or no medical training. This often led to severe loss of blood, other complications or infections that were untreatable until after the advent of penicillin. Most suffered excruciating pain and many of those who survived were subsequently unable to have children. It is impossible to guess with any accuracy what impact this incident had, not just on Angela but also on her relationship with John. Nor is it possible to guess whether he knew what had happened or whether she told any of her family. It is just as likely she may have endured this ordeal on her own, or simply told her sister Joan with whom she was always very close. I think it is probable that she kept this information to herself otherwise her family would have secured an abortion by another means. It was not unusual for young women from well-to-do or professional backgrounds to have family contacts who could secure an abortion by open-minded gynaecologists under the pretence of sorting out problems with irregular periods. This traumatic experience and the physical damage it caused may explain why later she had no children of her own. It is likely it may even have had a destructive impact on her relationship with John; perhaps she was already beginning to realise that he was unable to give her the support she needed. It is almost certain that it had a long lasting emotional and physiological impact, sufficient for her to include reference to it within her autobiography some 50 years later and tell others later in life of her ordeal.

John had certainly swept her off her feet and when subsequently they married in 1933 and Angela moved into his flat in Worcester Terrace, it is evident that she was already having doubts about their suitability for each other, as events in the years leading up to their marriage indicate. He had been only too ready to visit Russia in the summer of 1931 and returned 'more vocal than ever on Marxist theory' but to Angela's exasperation he refused to join the Communist Party or any other left-wing organisation.

Worcester Terrace, Clifton, as it is now

Angela Remembered

—3—
Militancy, Marriage and Marxism

Whilst Pilley continued to theorise, meanwhile much to his annoyance, Angela joined and became active within the Communist Party and was soon organising meetings, acting as a driver, attending meetings and becoming 'legal observer' at demonstrations, including facing baton charges by the police at two violent demonstrations in Bristol in 1932. It would be charitable to conclude that Pilley was merely attempting to protect Angela but I think it more likely that he was trying to mould her into his image of how his future wife should behave. Angela was never going to allow herself to be consigned to a subservient role and domesticity held no allure. Clearly they were both strong personalities, both used to being the centre of attention, and it is tempting to conclude that there were too many tensions in their relationship for a happy ending.

In the early 1930s, driven by increasing unemployment, there was significant unrest across the country culminating in the formation of the National Unemployed Workers Movement and in Bristol this resulted in a significant number of marches and angry demonstrations. This unemployment was a direct result of the Wall Street Crash that had led the USA to call in loans and blockade imports from outside the States. This had a devastating impact on manufacturing in most other countries and the UK economy faltered resulting in workers being laid off, mass unemployment and families left destitute as benefits were cut.

The queues at the Labour Exchange were getting longer and as a solicitor Angela saw at first hand the financial problems that ordinary people were experiencing with high levels of unemployment, bankruptcies increasing and individuals losing everything and being forced into destitution. Those in key

positions within the Communist Party, including the eminent
political activist and Welsh organiser of the National
Unemployed Workers Movement, Lewis Jones, had questioned
why someone from such a prosperous middle class background,
what she called her 'unfortunate origins', would want to be
involved. There was no alternative for Angela; unlike others from
the moneyed classes she did not regard it as her duty, her
motivation was a growing sense of rage that there had to be a
better way.

Soon Angela, who was lucky enough to own a car, was in the
privileged position of driving Lewis Jones to attended numerous
meetings and rallies throughout Wales and the West Country. The
Trades Union Congress, held at Bristol's Victoria Rooms in
September of 1931, was a sparking point for trouble on
5 September. Preparations were already underway to enforce cuts
to benefits and the much-hated Means Test was due to be
imposed in October of that year. A delegation of the National
Unemployed Workers Movement from the Welsh Valleys
intended to make representations to the TUC and had marched
from South Wales under the banner of 'Struggle or Starve'.
However, on reaching the city outskirts they were met by
mounted police attempting unsuccessfully to turn them back.
They marched on to The Horsefair to hold a rally before
marching on to the TUC but just as their rally ended they were
baton charged by the police intent on breaking them up. Angela
noted that 'the fair minded Bristolians' were so angered by this
that the next day numbers grew from a few hundred to several
thousand and the police 'did not risk a second intervention on
that occasion'. Angela was surprised and incensed that despite the
justice of their cause the TUC refused them a hearing. She did
not question why the hearing was refused, nor that there might
have been a valid reason or alternative view, and might not have
listened if it did not concur with her own opinion of events. She
was an idealist for whom there was little room for compromise or
to accommodate a different interpretation from her own. History
tells a very different story. There was at the time a growing
hostility between the Communist Party and the unions who were
angered by these Communist Party fronted marches which

claimed to represent the unemployed at a time when most craft unions had strong Unemployed Sections and were perfectly capable of representing and campaigning for themselves. The constitution of the Trades Union Congress which was, and remains, a delegate-based conference to which members of the partner unions are elected as representatives, does not permit non-delegates to arrive and demand to speak. The leader of the march Wal (Walter) Hannington was a founder member of the Communist Party and National Organiser of the National Unemployed Workers Movement. Despite subsequently becoming a relatively high profile member of the Amalgamated Engineering Union, he was at the time making increasingly anti-union speeches and once even called on workers not to join a union. Matters were not helped by the Communist Party having an annual showcase march on the TUC, which as with all their marches, was deliberately aimed at provoking violent clashes with the police as part of a tactic to create a revolutionary movement.

Inevitably, once the cuts to benefits were imposed, the numbers of those without employment or any other means of support increased. They were abandoned and destitute; anger spread across the country resulting in mass demonstrations. There was a rapid rise in unemployment in Bristol as businesses closed, industrial workforces were being laid off and underground workers in the local coal pits were being sacked without notice. Despite attempts by the authorities in Bristol to ban meetings, there were two huge demonstrations in February 1932. Angela was present at both and from her memory of the second of these events stated that in Old Market Street an 'immense crowd' gathered and 'they were suddenly set upon by posses of police who had been hiding in shop doors and side alleys whilst mounted police charged up from Old Market Street and laid into them. There were seventy casualties, some needing hospital treatment. But, unfortunately for the police, this happened just as the Castle Street Cinema ended and the crowds came out. Amongst many of them who were also beaten up were a local journalist and his girlfriend who had been at the cinema. As a result the Bristol Evening Post account the following day was indeed vivid!' Angela was horrified by what she had seen.

Riot in Old Market, Bristol in 1932

Her legal expertise proved useful in defending the leaders of the
National Unemployed Workers Movement who had been
arrested for incitement. She was also 'frequently in demand in
South Wales where police violence was getting out of hand and
the courts were imposing savage sentences on demonstrators'.

One effect of these struggles was the development of the
Socialist League in 1932 with its aim of converting both the
workers and the unemployed to socialism. A strong branch was
created in Bristol in November of that year led by the
controversial Bristol East MP, Sir Stafford Cripps, who with
others, including two young members Angela and John, was
growing alarmed at the rise of fascism in Germany, with its
racialism, attacks on trade unions and civil liberties, and the threat
of war. Angela recounts how the University's Socialist Society
decided to lay a wreath on Armistice Day at the University's War
Memorial. It was customary for the University Officer Training
Corps to lay an official wreath there at the Remembrance Service.
She and John decided upon the wording, which was subsequently
agreed by the committee, as follows: "To the Dead of All
Nations, victims of a war they did not make, from those who are
pledged to fight against all such crimes of Imperialism."

The Vice-Chancellor ordered the removal of the wreath and
the caption was destroyed leading to angry protests and a

petition, but without success. Angela, John and their friends were baffled that ordinary people and even those in authority seemed oblivious to the impact the events taking place in Europe might have on world peace.

Although John had not approved of Angela's direct approach to politics and Angela was beginning to feel constrained by what she regarded as his political inactivity, the marriage took place and Angela moved into his home. No doubt they each thought that they could shape the other into a similar way of thinking, but that would have been optimistic given the strength of their characters. Perhaps after a long courtship they saw no alternative, or maybe they saw it as a new beginning. Windsor Terrace was a few minutes walk from her family home and just around the corner from her former school but her world and understanding of politics was about to change dramatically. Their relationship, once married, quickly began to deteriorate; she was not the ideal homemaker, having never accomplished the domestic arts of cooking and cleaning; and he obviously did not regard her as his intellectual equal and despised her lack of knowledge of Marxist theory. John had been one of the most promising students of his generation at Oxford and through him she met other gifted young Oxford graduates like Hugh Gaitskell, Richard Crossman and John Strachey and was initially impressed not just by his intelligence but his wide circle of influential friends. Angela, who was only twenty-three when they met, was perhaps a little infatuated with her older and more experienced lover and the glamorous new world of politics and academia to which she was being introduced. Few young and innocent girls could fail to be flattered by the attentions of such a worldly wise and stylish tutor.

Later, there were numerous visits to London so that John could have some 'intelligent conversation' in trendy Soho restaurants and large houses in Hammersmith with 'real intellectuals' like Sage (John Desmond) Bernal and Naomi Mitchison where those present would be 'hanging on every word about the meaning of revolutionary theory'. Angela found these 'dreary gatherings' incredibly boring. The prolonged theoretical conversations of the intellectuals with no proposals for action both puzzled and worried her as they bore no relationship to the everyday reality of the hardships people were experiencing. She recounts an amusing instance when she left one such meeting early to attend a mass demonstration at Hyde Park of Welsh and West Country Hunger Marchers. Bernal also made an excuse about another appointment and left. She joined a group of Londoners with banners marching to the demonstration only to discover him marching beside her, they grinned at each other, then shared a taxi back only to be 'met by raised eyebrows'.

It was at one of these gatherings that she first met the renowned politician, barrister and Soviet sympathiser DN (Denis Nowell) Pritt who like Angela did not find these meetings particularly enlightening. Meeting Pritt and being introduced to his wide circle of friends and colleagues was to be a turning point in her life and he recognised in her a sharp legal mind and an ability to organise. She subsequently worked with him on a number of cases and recalls one instance when he had been defending unemployed miners at Blaina in Monmouthshire who had been charged with 'riot and assault' after police with batons had been called to viciously break up a large demonstration. The miners were cleared of assault but convicted of riot and sent to gaol. Pritt was in a sombre and reflective mood on the drive back to Bristol and said he had gone down to the cells afterwards to apologise for having failed them but to his surprise they shook their heads and embraced him! She and John visited Pritt and his wife on many occasions at their country home on the Berkshire Downs. These gatherings were an opportunity to meet left-wing activists and intellectuals. Often foreign and international movement visitors as well as prominent socialists were in attendance and both Angela and John were enthused by the stimulating discussions. It was at one of these house parties that Angela first met the conscientious objector, author and journalist Robert Page Arnot, known to his friends as Robin, who had co-founded the Communist Party of Great Britain and Labour Monthly. It was the start of a friendship between Robin and Angela that was to last for the remainder of their lives.

John Pilley was a physicist and lecturer in the theory and method of science education at the University of Bristol. He shared Angela's left-wing principles but he apparently regarded her as too much the activist and she thought him an intellectual theorist. She recounts that on many occasions he questioned why she spent so much time organising and following the unemployed in preference to studying Marxist theory. He had even offered to send her to the Lenin School in Moscow for six months to learn first hand about Marxism but she felt that she could do more by using her skills in Britain to improve the lives of others. Perhaps to distract her, John Pilley entered her name in a newspaper competition to receive flying lessons, and to her surprise she won. It was a new challenge that she greatly enjoyed, receiving lessons at the Bristol Airfield just off the Wells Road and was allowed to fly solo after less than 5 hours flying time and after less than 16 flying hours she took her test and passed. She remembered flying low over her sister's cottage at The Rookery, Dundry near Bristol. A report in the Bristol Evening Times of these exploits describes Angela as 'a striking personality with hair neatly cropped, vivacious manner, Miss Tuckett is an attractive representative of the modern age' and quotes her own description of these flying experiences as 'It was all so simple'. I imagine her, as in everything she undertook, to be a quick learner and an intrepid pilot. Unfortunately, it was too expensive both in time and money for her to continue this hobby and John was now using another diversionary tactic, inviting her to join him on trips abroad during university vacations. Surely this must have been more alluring for an eager young woman looking for adventure? It was certainly without hesitation that she joined her husband on numerous expeditions throughout Europe.

When she was in her early twenties, her father tracing links with their family's origins in Cornwall, had taken Angela to Brittany and she had become a regular visitor to Jersey on camping holidays with school friends and neighbours. She had, as a result of these early excursions, rapidly developed a taste for the excitement of overseas travel. She found these expeditions exhilarating and relished every opportunity to broaden her knowledge of the world, but as her experience of international sporting and other events will reveal, she also found these experiences challenging and at times dangerous.

Angela Remembered

–4–
Sport, Overseas Travel and Taking Risks

Throughout the late 1920s and 30s Angela travelled widely across Europe and to USA but most notably during the Spanish Civil War as an activist and propagandist in support of the Spanish Republic. There were visits to the South of France, Corsica, Spain, Greece and Cyprus. In those days of fast emerging fascism Angela was only too aware of the growing economic, political, racial and national tensions.

Angela, always a keen sportswoman, had begun playing hockey at a senior level in 1926 for Gloucester, known as The County Wanderers, and in 1928 for The West, when in 1929 she was part of an official tour to Frankfurt, Hamburg and Copenhagan. She won praise for speed as right wing and accuracy of shooting. She was promoted in the 1931 season to play for England and that year, playing against Ireland in Dublin, there was one incident at a formal dinner after a match when the Irish Captain from Ulster had raised a glass 'Ladies — The King'. The English visitors with the exception of Angela rose to their feet but half the Irish, which included players from Ulster, Munster and Leinster remained seated with their arms folded. She was congratulated by some of the Irish team members but needed to explain that as a Communist her opposition was to any monarchy! There was no repetition of this incident when they next played Ireland in Cork where there could be no loyal toast!

A story that has often been repeated to me was that Angela had competed in the 1936 Olympics as a member of the British Hockey Team and unlike her fellow competitors refused to give the Nazi salute to Hitler. It is alleged that she attempted, unsuccessfully, to dissuade her teammates from saluting Hitler and becoming part of the propaganda machinery validating the

Nazi regime. The story continues that the Nazis were furious at this slight and thereafter she was dropped from the team and never played hockey for her country again.

This subsequently proved to be not exactly true since hockey was not an Olympic sport at that time. The reality behind this anecdote is in many ways much more interesting. She did indeed play hockey for England and was part of a team that played in a tournament in Germany in 1935 in a stadium designed and being made ready for the Olympics the following year. Angela was horrified that the Nazis viewed this event as a mechanism to gain publicity for their regime. Wherever the team went press and cameras surrounded them as they prepared for 'the big match' on 14 April. Unusually for a women's hockey match there was a crowd of more than a thousand including several groups of uniformed troops. Hitler was not present but he had sent General von Blomberg, who was at that time the Commander in Chief of the armed forces, as his deputy. The English team had to pass through a cordon of the Hitler youth all giving the Nazi salute as they entered the stadium. Obviously Angela did not return their salute. She recounts that it was a 'hard fought match' but that they won and that afterwards the press surrounded them, wanting to find out what the English players thought of the 'new Germany'. Angela, left on her own with the press, was evasive and was only prepared to give an account of the game and tactics and refused to answer their questions that were seeking support for the new Germany. An escort from the British Embassy asked her to find someone to speak to the German press 'who does not have, shall we say, your scruples'. The next day when travelling by train to play in Holland, she was told that complaints had been received at the highest level about her behaviour and she was reprimanded by a hostile team manager. It is easy to understand why in 1935 the British diplomats and team officials had taken this stance. Britain's leaders at the time were keen to appease Germany and a naval agreement was reached that same year. Regardless of Germany's contempt for the Treaty of Versailles signed after the First World War, which they had already broken, the British Government mistakenly saw Hitler not so much as a threat but as a possible ally against Russia. Despite having been one of the most successful players in the team, playing International Hockey from 1931 until 1935, she was never again selected to play for England, even as a reserve.

Having been excluded from playing hockey for her country, John Pilley, by now her husband of three years, suggested in the spring of 1936 that she should join him on a lecture tour of the Greek Islands with eminent archaeologists John Myers and Stanley Casson. It was for Angela, who was also a keen swimmer, not so much an archaeological expedition but 'a beautiful holiday in beautiful places'. In Athens at the start of the tour she was amazed to see so many political slogans with hammer and sickle symbols painted on the high walls in the poorer and working class areas of the city. Things changed dramatically, not just for Angela but also for the world, in the summer of 1936. John Pilley's father had persuaded him to go with him on a trip to USA in July in the hope of improved job prospects and she was alone in Bristol.

Early that summer the fascist Greek dictator Metaxas seized power, meanwhile in Spain Franco started his rebellion against the Spanish Popular Front Government, with the support of Hitler in Germany and Mussolini in Italy. The impact of this was immense and later at Guernica, Angela 'was to see for the first time ever, civilians in a country town being bombed from the air, and from Nazi planes'. Angela pleaded with the right wing Labour Councillor and Secretary of Bristol Trades Council, EH Parker, to set up a Committee for the Defence of Spanish Democracy. His response was that no one would be interested. However, others in the city were of a different mind-set. A Spanish Committee, disgusted at the Chamberlain government policy of non-intervention, was formed and the words of a petition agreed. Volunteers met night and day in an office above a photographer's shop in Park Street organising meetings, demonstrations and other activities to raise awareness of what was happening in Spain. Their slogan was 'Bombs on Barcelona mean Bombs on Bristol'.

When John returned to Bristol from his visit to USA that autumn he found Angela exhausted from campaigning and persuaded her to join him on a second lecture tour of the Greek Islands in the spring of 1937. They stopped off in Paris where they met with what Angela described contemptuously as 'young London left-wing intelligentsia on their way back from Moscow'. She was right to be dismissive. They were on a mission to take some aid money to Greece where it was greatly needed but preferred to go straight back to London and suggested Angela and John should take the money instead. Despite an argument between John, who didn't want the responsibility, and Angela who thought it was their duty, it was agreed that they would take the money to Athens. When they arrived in Piraeus Harbour the shop to which they intended to deliver the money appeared almost permanently shut. There was another argument and John said it had been a mistake from the start. Angela, in 'a flaming rage' by now decided to go on her own to the streets at the foot of the Acropolis where on a previous visit she had seen Communist slogans. These had now been covered with whitewash. She sat dejectedly down on the kerb in the dusty and deserted street where a small group of children were playing and they soon began to show an interest in her. She pointed at the patch on the wall where the slogan had been then traced a hammer and sickle in the dust with her finger and made the sign of a clenched fist. One of the older children understood immediately and took her hand leading her to a nearby house where a woman took her in her arms, gave her some wine and introduced her to a man who spoke some French. Angela, fluent in French, explained the difficulty and asked him if he could contact the shop-keeper as it was 'extremely important for the comrades that she should be found'. She went on to say that it was essential they came to their boat in the harbour as they would be sailing at midnight. Angela at first waited patiently, then with increasing agitation but to her relief, shortly before the boat sailed, the shopkeeper, an English woman, and her American girl assistant appeared with armfuls of flowers ostensibly to see them off. They were taken down to their cabin, Angela explained that the money was Red Aid and gave it to the women who assured her it would reach the right quarter. The American girl later returned to the United States and Angela met her there briefly the following year.

—5—
Conflict and Farewells

When John and Angela returned to England he received the offer of a year's sabbatical at New York University. Although there were numerous difficulties in the marriage and he had not been faithful, she felt that a change of environment might result in a fresh start and reluctantly agreed to go with him. His extramarital relationships had been casual affairs, or so she thought, but even as Angela said farewell to family and friends, he was in Paris with the woman who was to become his second wife.

On 27 August 1937 John and Angela took the train to Liverpool to catch the boat to New York. He was 37 and she was 31. Angela described it as 'an extremely unhappy journey'. Even as the train left Bristol they were no longer speaking to each other and once they had embarked she quickly realised her error and wished she had remained in England. She considered leaving the ship at Cork but she had no money and any thoughts she had of joining her brother in partnership at her father's legal firm were subsequently dashed when only 6 weeks after leaving England her father died unexpectedly and her brother needed to take on a new partner as a matter of urgency. Angela, for the first time in her life, felt entirely alone and was without any occupation or means of earning money.

However, just before leaving England Angela had gone to the London HQ of the Communist Party where she met Tom Mann, by then an old man, who gave her some letters to deliver in America to friends within the American Communist Party. She says of the meeting that 'the old man held my hands and looked at me for a long time, before embracing me'. He told her that he had known and greatly admired her Aunt Enid. He remembered her as a brilliant speaker who knew how to make her voice heard.

Angela, on arrival in New York, delivered these letters to the Communist Party offices from which she discovered that an immense demonstration was about to take place and was due to march on the Japanese Embassy in protest at the seizure of Manchuria. She ran down the streets and arrived close to the front of the demonstration and was enthralled by the spectacle of the crowd with banners and flags but equally surprised to see, very prominently displayed, a massive flag with a pole at each side – the Stars and Stripes. She later learned that any demonstration, which failed to display the national flag, was deemed illegal. One pole was thrust into the hand of a young black girl who worked in a local clothing factory and Angela, to her surprise, was chosen to carry the other pole because she looked so fresh and all-American! 'So within two days of setting foot on American soil, there I was taking part in leading several thousand protestors up New York's Fifth Avenue.' Initially excited by New York, Angela soon discovered that the university circles in which she was mixing were even duller than in the UK and many aspects of life in America puzzled and perplexed her.

The relationship between this ill-matched and unhappy couple began to decline further and between the inevitable rows they were becoming more remote from each other. It is apparent that she was not simply bored with her new life in America but also lonely and desperate for something to occupy the hours. She made contact first with the Society for Cultural Relations with the Soviet Union but found it was 'rather more cultural than socialist'.

She thought the North American Committee for Spanish Relief was more plausible but discovered that its function was to hold 'too many money raising cocktail parties'. Undaunted she continued to look for an organisation that would fill the void and soon found herself arranging a sale of authors' manuscripts for the League of American Writers to raise aid for the Spanish struggles. She rapidly made friends with a number of left-wing writers and was impressed by the radical theatre productions she saw in New York, especially Marc Blitzstein's musical The Cradle Will Rock, so much so that she sang the opening song A Nickle Under Your Foot into a greetings disc machine and sent it to her sister Joan who was delighted with it when it arrived home in England.

The political situation in Europe was becoming more volatile and war seemed inevitable. It was much on Angela's mind. John had secured a second year's sabbatical to go to Wellesley College in Boston, Massachusetts, but they returned briefly to England in 1938 to make ready for his new appointment. Just before returning to USA Angela attended the Communist Party Congress in Birmingham which coincided with the 'Munich Betrayal', the agreement between Nazi Germany, France, Italy and UK which enabled Germany to take over the German speaking areas of Czechoslovakia. On her return to America, Angela's friends in the League of American Writers welcomed her back to New York. Meanwhile in the Mid-West John had orchestrated another betrayal. Angela's replacement, his future wife, had been invited to work with him there for a while.

Throughout the two years in America, Angela had maintained a lively correspondence with DN Pritt, who was at the time struggling to write an analysis of Mein Kampf. They were now able to exchange comments on the reaction to political events on both sides of the Atlantic. The situation in all respects was bleak. Early in 1939 whilst she was still in the States he wrote: 'I was approached recently to know whether I would write a short explanation of Marxism in words of one syllable for the bourgeoisies to understand, for mammoth circulation. I replied that I knew someone else who could. Would you like to do it? When you return? Under cover of my name, ie you write it in English and then I translate it into Prittish?' This Penguin book project was soon shelved as the prospect of conflict in Europe grew even closer.

The potential for a war in Europe created personal problems for Angela. Many of the English then living in America were seeking to evade war by remaining in USA but this did not suit Angela. John Pilley was invited to stay a year longer at Wellesley College whilst the University of Bristol urged him to return. Unable to decide he apparently agreed to both. Angela, who had just learnt of John's duplicity, and recognising that her marriage was over, was more decisive. So in July of 1939 she left New

York by ship to return home to Britain. Of these unequal partners in an unhappy marriage it seems that Angela was the stronger and more resolute of the two. A still undecided John arrived back in Britain in August and rented a small flat at Lambs Conduit Street in Holborn, having previously re-let their home in Bristol, leaving Angela to find her own accommodation. Initially she stayed with her sister Joan but after a few weeks moved to London to share a flat with Robin and Olive Arnot's daughter Barbara and started looking for jobs. Meanwhile, John was persuaded to return to America. Angela moved into his small London flat and two years later she divorced him for desertion.

Politics had proved to be a heady aphrodisiac but not sufficient to sustain a relationship in which one party not only regards the other as intellectually inferior but also has affairs outside the marriage. Many of Pilley's students were devoted to him and interestingly Angela explains in her autobiography that he 'shared their devotion' and that one subsequently set up home with him, became his second wife and mother of his two sons. John Pilley was clearly flattered by the attentions of his young female students and it seems likely that he exploited this to his own advantage. Angela had been deeply attracted to Pilley when they first met and she learnt much from his knowledge of world history and politics. He was also able to introduce her to others who were to have a profound influence on her future. She soon became disillusioned but despite the difficulties of their marriage, she had tried to make it work, so the hurt of betrayal must have been all the harder to bear.

Yet, perhaps surprisingly, when John Pilley returned from USA in 1951 as Professor of Education at the University of Edinburgh, he and his new wife remained on friendly terms with Angela. They continued to correspond with each other until his death in 1968, regularly meeting with Angela on her many visits to Scotland to carry out research on behalf of DN Pritt and into several books she had been commissioned to write.

—6—
Bristol Unity Players

Both Angela and her sister Joan were members of the League of Progressive Writers. Joan had trained at the Royal Academy of Dramatic Art, appeared as Ophelia to Forbes Robertson's Hamlet, and was a good friend of George Bernard Shaw having appeared in his play Caesar and Cleopatra in London, They were stalwarts of Bristol's Unity Players Club, of which Joan was producer, from 1935 until 1947 co-writing plays `The Bulls see Red', `Passing Unnoticed', `Smash and Grab', `Aiden & Abetten' and `Charity Begins' as well as music for productions. There had been a number of workers dramatic societies in the Bristol area in the early 1930s and these were brought together by Joan to form the Unity Players in 1935. The Players continued to liaise with various left-wing organisations in the city and beyond, including the Left Book Club's Theatre Guild and the London Unity Theatre. Despite frequent air raids and casualties within the players, the club continued to put on performances throughout the Second World War and only ceased due to falling membership and Joan's failing health. Joan died in 1957 after many years of being severely disabled with rheumatoid arthritis. Later in 1979 Angela wrote a pamphlet entitled The People's Theatre in Bristol 1930 – 1945 for the Communist Party of Great Britain and in 1980 deposited various documents including scripts, programmes and photographs relating to the Unity Players with the University of Warwick's Theatre Studies Department. In the pamphlet she states that 'Bristol Unity Players was an early attempt to build an audience for a people's theatre which would be a social voice and a social force for change'.

Olga Shotton, now in her 80s, knew Angela well and remembers her and her family from childhood right up until and

OUR HISTORY PRICE 45p

PAMPHLET 72

THE PEOPLE'S THEATRE IN BRISTOL 1930-45

BY ANGELA TUCKETT

after Angela's death. She said the Tucketts were a very talented family of left wing socialists. Olga's own parents Hilda and Eric Crompton, like Angela and her sister Joan, were members of both the Communist Party of Great Britain and the Unity Players in Bristol. Indeed, Eric Crompton who had been imprisoned as a conscientious objector, breaking rocks on Dartmoor during the First World War, was the founder of the Communist Party in Bristol. Olga remembers being taken to meetings in Bristol where her own family and the Tucketts were present and that she always cringed when her tone-deaf father sang the Internationale more loudly than anyone else! Olga had been roped in as a small child to help with the Unity Players during the Spanish Civil War. Yet she remembers to this day the first line of one play 'In the merry month of May, Spain lies bleeding'.

Joan Tuckett like her sister was widely travelled, touring and performing in USA and Canada but returned to teach drama in Manchester and subsequently Bristol where she worked with various theatre groups which became the foundation of the Unity Players. She was to remain in the Bristol area throughout the remainder of her life, sharing a cottage with sculptor Doris Flinn and her friend Bridget Fitzsimon who were also members of the Unity Players. According to Olga, Bridget nursed her at her home in Dundry in the final years before her death in 1957 by which time Joan had become bedridden.

The Unity Players performed in theatres and prominent public places including Colston Hall and open-air stages on The Downs and in Queen Square, attended by thousands and always in protest or in celebration of some significant event in the socialist calendar. In one production Olga told me that the children, herself included, were seen playing with bricks and at the end had to arrange them into the words 'Unite for Peace' at the front of the stage.

Angela Remembered

—7—
The War and Recovery

Once John had returned to America, Angela needed to support herself and her first job, although far from ideal, was as a finance clerk in a large office where she quickly discovered how hierarchical such places were and that a culture of bullying existed openly in the workplace. Always a feisty woman she stood up to the bullying and as she was already a trade union member she encouraged others to join. This did not please the management and it wasn't long before she received a letter saying her services were no longer required. Unhappy in this workplace where the role of women was subservient, despite the need to employ more women in traditional male roles during the war, and with no opportunity for progression, she left without any resistance. It would have caused her concern that nearly a century later most women are still unequal in the workplace and suffer lack of respect, economic inequality and bullying. She had joined the National Amalgamated Workers Union on taking her first job in her father's office. It was still known to its members by its original name as The Workers' Union, even though it had merged in 1929 with various dock and transport workers unions to become Britain's largest amalgamated union, The Transport and General Workers Union, now Unite. It was partly through her connections with this union that she was commissioned later in her life to write a history of 'The Scottish Carter'.

The war had just begun and it was not long before bombs began to fall on London but Angela, fearless as ever, was unrelenting in her decision to remain in the city. She had been doing voluntary advice work on Sundays with a group of Communist Party lawyers for the Daily Worker and Bill Rust, its editor, a friend and a Communist activist, suggested Angela might like to join the National Council for Civil Liberties. She was an ideal candidate and was appointed Head of the Legal Department of the National Council for Civil Liberties (now Liberty) in 1940. She was not only well read but had always enjoyed writing and it was a natural progression for someone with a legal training, sharp mind, good judgement, astute understanding of politics and belief in equality. Angela immersed herself in her new role. It was not an easy job, and with so many different organisations evacuated to the country, people were constantly seeking advice on a range of different matters, from work related issues to providing guidance on the Wartime Defence Regulations and giving assistance to refugees who were bring treated as enemy aliens. Whilst there she wrote a pamphlet 'Civil Liberty and the Industrial Worker' published in 1942 about the numerous restrictions imposed on workers involved in wartime defence contracts.

The bombing rapidly grew fiercer and many who had initially intended to stay in London now moved out to the country and sought caretakers for their homes. Angela was approached by a friend to look after a house near Victoria Station and gave up the tenancy of her flat but just before she was due to move it was heavily bombed. Instead she moved to St John's Wood where several of her friends, also in key roles in London, had gathered. During the heavy night bombing they kept themselves occupied discussing the war, politics and Marxist theory.

DN Pritt was amongst the regular visitors as he was frequently unable to travel home to his country house and there was much discussion between him and Angela about abuses of power, of which there were only too many, in relation to the Defence Regulations. Unfair detention without any explanation or trial being commonplace, and even when there was a hearing, it was in secret with no right to a legal advisor, and questions were being raised about the freedom of the press. One woman had been detained for five months simply for handing out pamphlets explaining how to become a conscientious objector. A new Anti-Strike Regulation was introduced and people were being victimised simply for expressing an adverse opinion or comment. Anyone with pacifist views, even prominent ministers of religion, was banned from speaking on the BBC and Sir Hugh Roberton was barred from conducting the Glasgow Orpheus Choir. Angela's workload unsurprisingly was increasing and she now had 584 open cases.

Bombings previously only in cover of darkness began to take place in the daytime and Angela recorded in her diary that 'The war came to our doorstep – and indeed it did not stop there: it knocked at our doors and windows which courteously gave way… In traditional Liberty style we registered a strong protest by continuing to defend civil liberties here and now'. She continues that the Legal Department 'paused merely to stuff the old shirt of a predecessor into the window, flicked the more noticeable slivers of glass from the chair seats (to avoid claims for damages from callers) and plunged again into arrears of Cases Reported'. Ronald Kidd, Civil Rights campaigner and founder of National Council for Civil Liberties, thought her account 'too lighthearted' given the potential for a more serious incident.

The offices of the National Council for Civil Liberties had been forced to move and had relocated to Sloane Square, and Angela, finding cycling there from St John's Wood each day too complicated in war torn London, moved closer to work to a flat in Kings Road. She shared this small flat with a former student she had known in Bristol who had been conscripted to work in a London factory, and she started taking classes in Marxism. Had they still been together, John Pilley would no doubt have applauded this decision as he had spent many years encouraging her to learn more about the theory behind Marxist doctrine.

Angela's stay with the National Council for Civil Liberties was short lived, her enormous caseload over two years was crushing, and she joined the staff of The Daily Worker as its solicitor and legal advisor in 1942 working also as a reporter and subsequently sub-editor. She also needed to change trade unions and joined the NUJ — National Union of Journalists. The Daily Worker, the voice of the Communist Party of Great Britain, was banned in 1941 for what was regarded as its subversive activities. It had refused to be critical of Nazi Germany since Hitler had signed a non-aggression pact with Stalin and Soviet Russia in 1939. However, by 1942 when Angela joined the team, since the pact had been broken by Germany's invasion of the Soviet Union and The Daily Worker was openly hostile to Hitler, the Labour Government lifted the ban on the newspaper.

Angela in her autobiography describes 'having to learn new skills in a new industry' and remembers 'how frequently morning editorial conferences — when everyone criticised the day's paper and made proposals — would be interrupted by raids, including our first experience of the missile, the flying bomb from the French shore. The practice was for us to stay put, perhaps go down to the yard or merely drop under the table'. The paper's previous offices at Clayton Street had been totally destroyed by fire during one bombing raid and by now they were located in Swinton Street and much later moved to Farringdon Road. She recounts how it was necessary, as with all newspapers at that time, for certain stories to be taken to the Ministry prior to publication to ensure that there was nothing that might be of interest to the enemy.

Living within central London she was never far from the terror of frequent bombings and saw the horror at first hand. She told many distressing stories of the impact and intensity of war in her autobiography and the difficulty of facing the dead and helping the injured. She was in work on the morning of 6 August 1945 when she heard that the Americans had dropped their atomic bomb on Hiroshima and was one of the first to hear the news. It was to have a profound influence on her and thereafter she was more determined, as fear of nuclear war gripped the world, in her belief in peace and disarmament. Over a decade later in 1958 when the Campaign for Nuclear Disarmament was launched with a massive rally in London she joined the campaign.

But back in 1945 she was kept busy reporting on the many problems facing post-war London. The United Nations, formed that same year, necessitated a considerable amount of time and effort in attending meetings of the Security Council at Central Hall and writing numerous reports. Angela was also reporting on 'a major squatters occupation during the acute housing shortage', a 'phenomenal strike of catering workers at London's posh Savoy Hotel' as well as conferences of Fire Brigades and Public Sector Employees at Bournemouth and Worthing. Unexpectedly, the opportunity arose for her to visit Czechoslovakia, 'her first glimpse of a socialist country'. She was horrified by the amount of reconstruction required after the war and at the continuing racist attitude by many to the surviving Jewish people.

Life in post-war Britain was grim. She returned to England in 'the bitterly cold autumn of 1947, in ghastly weather with a desperate fuel shortage' and was immediately sent off to the docks to report on the much-anticipated arrival of the ships bringing coal from the northeast. It was the story of the moment in all the daily papers as Londoners were terrified that without coal they would be plunged into darkness and would die of cold with no means of heating or cooking food. The camaraderie amongst the many journalists 'smoking, drinking and yapping away' waiting for the arrival of the boats did not suit Angela. She preferred to befriend the dockworkers by indicating her hostility to the other journalists, mostly male. One crane driver, health and safety not being so keenly enforced at that time, even let an intrepid Angela climb up the steel framework and into his cab from which she had not only a birds-eye view of the docks but saw the coal ships as they came into view downstream.

The Daily Worker supported and helped organise several immense post-war gatherings. Paul Robeson was to be the guest of honour at one such event in the Harringay Arena in 1948, and Angela was looking forward to meeting him. Although forced to cancel he sent a recorded message of greeting that was received to 'thundered applause'. Later in 1950, just before he was investigated by McCarthy for his alleged Un-American Activities and prevented from leaving USA from 1950 until 1958 Angela was amongst the crowd of 6,000 who greeted him at a peace rally in Lincolns Inn Fields.

Through her friendship with Robin Page Arnot and his family she was privileged to meet and befriend Willie Gallacher, a regular visitor to their home. He had been one of the founding members of the Communist Party of Great Britain, whose notoriety came in part from his unswerving support of Stalin. He was at the time the MP for West Fife until he lost his seat in 1950. He was a Scottish trade unionist as well as a prolific writer and Angela found him to be an inspiration, very knowledgeable and of considerable assistance when she was working as a researcher on behalf of Robin Page Arnot in Scotland.

Angela continued to work for The Daily Worker until 1948 when she moved to Labour Monthly where she remained for another 30 years working as sub-editor to the writer and communist party theorist Rajani Palme Dutt. She wrote numerous articles and took it upon herself to reply to every letter readers submitted, and through the pages of the magazine 'their personalities and ideas became known to each other'. Angela states that in many cases it would have been 'impossibly unwise' to quote their real names as many contributors were from foreign countries or were in the forces and reprisals might have been taken against them. She published many of her readers' letters under pseudonyms including 'Canadian Lumber Jack', 'Inverness Airman' or simply 'Fernando'. Her articles and columns had wonderfully implicit titles such as 'Dollars – Without Strings!', 'On Not Being Beholden', 'Flourish the Trumpets', 'Press Lords and Strikers', 'The Sacred Trust', 'Behind the Times' and 'Undemocratic?'. It was here that she acquired an enviable reputation for writing succinct and cutting prose but also for her sense of humour. She attended many different conferences during these years and was always pleased and surprised when strangers would seize her hand and introduce themselves as one of her anonymous letter writers. Also, always ready to attend lobbies at the House of Commons, especially at times such as pit closures, the newspaper strike and the seamen and dockers dispute, she would ensure she had a good supply of Labour Monthly stashed in an unmarked bag to sell to ardent readers as well as those she felt needed to be converted! She also continued to sell the Daily Worker on Saturdays in Camden Town and at Chalk Farm tube station even after moving to 22 Woodside Grove, Finchley to 'share a house with local branch comrades'.

Angela became a regular visitor to Scotland from the 1950s onwards carrying out research, making notes and preparing drafts for RP Arnot's book 'A History of the Scottish Miners' published by Allen and Unwin in 1955. She developed a keen affinity for Scotland and thoroughly enjoyed her many visits which culminated in the commissioning and production of two of her own books, 'The Scottish Carter' published in 1967 and 'The Scottish Trades Union Congress: The First 80 Years 1897–1977' published in 1986. Her collaboration with Robert Arnot, who was already a prolific and respected writer, as his researcher continued for many years. They worked together on numerous books and pamphlets published under his name including writings on Bernard Shaw and William Morris.

Despite such a demanding job and hectic lifestyle Angela had still managed to find time for her own reading including most of the English classics, writing her diary each day, going to the theatre, attending regular concerts as well as folk song and music sessions in the pubs of Camden Town and Holborn where she met amongst others Ewan McColl and 'a shy young American singer', Peggy Seeger. She even found time to continue playing club hockey.

Angela's bravery in remaining in London throughout the war years together with her fearless and imaginative style of reporting on the events of the day combined with her professional and analytical approach is worthy of comment but is best summed up by one of her colleagues. Her long time friend and mentor Harry Pollitt who was General Secretary of the Communist Party of Great Britain for more than 20 years made the following statement on her 50th birthday, in January 1956, not long before his own death, that she 'brought to the Labour Movement her organising ability, fertile imagination and the power to take endless pains'.

Although her sister Joan had been an invalid for many years, her death in 1957 was still a devastating blow. Several years older than Angela, she was the closest person she had to a mother, and someone with whom she could share confidences. She wondered what the future held but would not have expected that in a few years she would be making another momentous move out of London and back to the West Country. In the mean time she continued to work as hard as ever. Throughout her years in London Angela played an active part in the London Trades Council to which she was a delegate, and various of its subsequent off-shoots, and on moving to Swindon took an equally energetic role in the activities of Swindon Trades Council.

Angela Remembered

−8−
The Swindon Years

Angela and Ike at their home in Liddington Street, Swindon.

Angela would probably have remained in London and continued working full time for Labour Monthly, which she later described as one of the 'extraordinarily rich periods' in her life, had she not met and married Irving Gradwell, known as Ike, in 1962. This opened an entirely new chapter in an already extraordinary life and they remained together until his death in 1979. She moved to Swindon at this point but at first, until 1963, retained her London flat as she initially continued to work for Labour Monthly. Throughout her life, even when living abroad and in London, she had never severed her links with Bristol and this move to Swindon brought her closer to old friends and family.

It was a second marriage for them both and they lived at 5 Liddington Street. Those who knew them from that time variously described them as 'soul-mates', 'like-minded', 'passionate' and 'a devoted couple' not just to each other but equally committed to the various causes they supported and shared. They were both strong personalities, each with a dogged determination to fight for the principles they had in common, but equally kind to each other, sharing a sense of humour and understanding of each other's needs, which may explain why their relationship was such a success. It was a marriage of equals.

They had met in 1961 when both Ike and his daughter Judith were on a visit to Czechoslovakia to which Angela had also been invited. The three of them instantly became friends and Angela stated that after the trip 'it seemed a pity to part', so they married the following year. She was invited on an official visit to the USSR in 1962 and as they were now married she was

Angela and Ike sitting in a square on one of their visits abroad

permitted by the authorities to take her new husband with her.

Ike was a Swindon based joiner and craft teacher, who was an activist within the NUT, Swindon Communist Party and the Peace Movement. Like Angela, Ike was born in 1906, on the 18 October, and though their family backgrounds were entirely different they had many other things in common. They both had indefatigable energy combined with intelligence and a quick mind, a desire to work hard and influence others and shared belief in a better system in which peace and equality were paramount. They were each legendary campaigners against fascism, which in Ike's case began long before he met Angela when he worked with Swindon's Railway Works activists in preparing and fitting out motorcycle ambulances to send to Spain during the Civil War. He was also instrumental in creating a Unity Bookshop in Swindon and during the Cold War in campaigning for peace through Swindon Peace Council. During the Second World War, as a skilled craftsman, he was deployed to work at Short's aircraft factory and then Marine Mountings (Listers) where he became an AEU (Amalgamated Engineering Union) shop steward.

The Communist Party in Swindon was particularly strong for a provincial town but there is a definite correlation between the strength of the party and the need for skilled engineering workers during the Second World War in the various industries associated with the production of military hardware. Some were evacuated from London and others brought in from different parts of the country to work in the necessary trades. Existing members such as Ike Gradwell actively recruited many of these workers into the Communist Party. Indeed the party was so successful in Swindon that in 1944 it was awarded a special commendation as

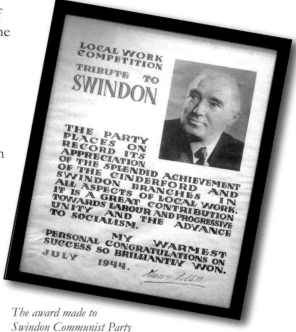

The award made to
Swindon Communist Party

part of a Local Work Competition for its achievements that it shared with Cinderford in Gloucestershire. The certificate, evocative of a bygone era, contains a photograph of Harry Pollitt, General Secretary of the Communist Party of Great Britain and is signed by him.

Ike's mother Lizzie Irving was a dressmaker and his father Septimus Gradwell a skilled joiner who lived in Ulverston in the Lake District. Although Ike had ambition and had won a scholarship to a local Grammar School, the financial means of his parents were such that he had no alternative but to follow his father into the joinery trade and was apprenticed to a joiner and undertaker – his memories of which were the source of many comical stories which he told with great hilarity. He had always been a keen sportsman and fate intervened when he was signed to play professional Rugby League by Hull Kingston Rovers. This change in fortune enabled him to pay his way through night school with the signing-on fee and qualify as a handicrafts teacher, working first in Suffolk and subsequently Swindon where he moved in 1935. He joined the Swindon Communist Party in 1936, becoming a key figure within it and its charismatic leader for many years, during which time he stood, albeit unsuccessfully, for Parliament in 1964 and 1966. His first wife Ethel died in 1957 leaving him to raise three teenage children on his own. It was their daughter Judith to whom Angela became stepmother, and according to many she treated as her own daughter, and assisted her in campaigning when Judith stood in the 1969 by-election and subsequently the following General Election. The two older children had already left home and the youngest, Judith was at university by the time Angela moved in permanently to live with Ike. Although Judith returned to Swindon ready for the election campaign and to take up a post in the planning department of the local council she perhaps wisely to avoid any friction did not return to the family home but found accommodation near her work.

Officially now retired as a journalist, Angela was made a Life Member of the National Union of Journalists in May 1966 in recognition of her long association with the union. Never afraid to commit pen to paper, she was a regular and outspoken contributor to the letters pages of various local and national newspapers. But she was equally critical and often outspoken within and about the various different organisations to which she belonged when she felt they were not sufficiently proactive in their campaigns.

Angela and Ike campaigning in Swindon: Picture by the Swindon Advertiser

Political activities not only continued once Angela had moved to Swindon but she became even more fervent in promoting the Communist cause, especially at local level. She became actively involved in local politics, standing as a Communist in the Wiltshire Council elections in 1967. She failed to win but surprisingly succeeded in gaining 7.4% of the poll, which, in a town then dominated by Labour and a county dominated by the Conservatives, was no mean feat.

Like her aunt Enid Stacy, Angela was a persuasive speaker and indefatigable campaigner. She galvanised support for her stepdaughter Judith Gradwell who stood as the Communist Party Candidate in the controversial Swindon by-election held on 3 October 1969. This followed the resignation of Labour MP Francis Noel-Baker and resulted in the election of Christopher Ward, a Conservative with 16,843 votes, a margin of just 478 votes. This election result together with other by-elections that year led to the defeat of Harold Wilson's government. Many in the Labour Party were unforgiving of the Communist Party in Swindon for having fielded a candidate and some rancour still remained for many years, even to this day. The Labour Party blamed the local Communists and the Gradwells for the efficiency of a campaign that resulted in Judith winning 518 votes. The Labour Candidate David Stoddart polled 16,365 votes but had Judith Gradwell not stood many thought it more than likely that David Stoddart would have been elected. My view is that this argument is flawed. We live in a democratic society in which Judith was entitled to stand for election. Had she not exercised that right there is no guarantee that those who voted for her would have voted Labour as an alternative. This was an extraordinary result by anyone's estimation and it is indicative of the esteem in which the Gradwell family was held that Judith achieved so many votes. Several people I spoke to, who were not members of the Communist Party, said that after this event there was resentment to Angela's prominence in other non-party political campaigns. They felt that the general public regarded her as so left-wing that they would not listen to the socialist message, however reasonable or important it may have been. David Stoddart subsequently won the seat in the General Election of

Campaigning with members of Swindon Communist Party, June 1975

the following year and continued to hold the seat until 1989. Judith Gradwell polled slightly less that year with 456 votes. They say that whichever party wins in Swindon wins the general election but in 1970 this was not the case and to the surprise of many Edward Heath formed the Conservative Government that year.

Angela had rapidly become an indispensable part of the campaigning machinery within the town and was regularly seen alongside Ike and other members of the party taking part in various demonstrations, at meetings and at exhibitions. Wherever there was a call seeking support for one campaign or another, she was there. She actively campaigned with Ike for peace during the cold war, defended striking miners and sought contributions to their strike funds during various miners' strikes but especially during the 'Three Day Week' of 1974 and 1975 and supported public sector workers during the 'Winter of Discontent' of 1978 to 1979.

When Ike died on 6 February 1979, he and Angela were staying in his daughter Judith's house in Bristol where Judith was now working. He hadn't been well and Angela and Judith were both present when he died. Angela noted in her diary with some sadness that Ike had only recently before his death delivered a typically confident and hard-hitting speech, but she also noted how desolate and alone she now felt.

Olga Shotton who had known Angela in Bristol knew very little of Angela's first husband but Angela told her that Ike Gradwell, her second, was 'the love of her life'. Olga said 'Angela was terribly fond of him, in fact she adored him, and was devastated when he died'. She also told me that Angela was very proud and fond of her stepdaughter Judith Gradwell who had worked for Bristol City Council and subsequently Bath and North East Somerset in the planning department looking after public footpaths; something that Angela's own father had cherished as the founder of the South West of England Footpaths Preservation Society.

Several people have told me that Angela's fondness for her stepdaughter was not necessarily reciprocal and that theirs was a strained relationship. Angela was used to having her own way and a number of people told me that she did not enjoy being contradicted by anyone, no matter what the circumstances. The

Angela and Ike taking election nomination papers to Swindon Borough Council circa 1970

bond between natural mothers and their daughters is not always perfect and can be competitive and controlling. The stereotype of the wicked stepmother is a caricatured image familiar to most and probably derives from what must by necessity be a difficult and complex relationship. It is therefore understandable that there must have been tensions between the two women. A strong and determined woman, such as Angela, would not have been afraid to voice her feelings and could have proved a difficult adversary.

This tension between stepmother and stepdaughter was confirmed when I met Judith Gradwell who told me that she was 16 years old when her father remarried and as with any family there were occasional differences of opinion, but that Angela could be very difficult 'she didn't do shades of grey, she always saw everything in black and white', something I had observed for myself on a number of occasions. However, Judith never quarrelled with Angela, though they may have suppressed their feelings, as they both loved Ike and neither would have wanted to do anything that would have upset him. Several people had previously told me that Angela was an idealist and could be extremely stubborn never accepting that she might be in the wrong! It could not have been easy for a young woman, even though she had left the family home, to have another woman who she hardly knew take becoming her stepmother. Especially such a determined person as Angela, who was clearly not a natural home maker and had no experience of motherhood either in her own right as a mother, or through the love of her own mother who she never knew. It was just as well that Angela did not permanently move from her flat in London to live with Ike until Judith left home to go to university in 1963. However, it was a relief for Judith that there was someone to look after her father when she was away, as she had been torn between going to university and leaving her father on his own.

Judith said Ike and Angela had a really good life together and she was very pleased that they were so happy. Many, Judith included, saw Angela not simply as very glamorous, but she had done everything — from playing hockey for her country to influencing others through her writing and politics. She was regarded as the perfect match for Ike and someone who was central to the various local political campaigns they undertook together. Judith's theory is that as Angela grew older and her glamour faded she had difficulty coping with no longer being the centre of attention. This, combined with the fact that most of us in varying degrees become more cantankerous as we age, must have affected the way she interacted with her stepdaughter and others. The relationship between stepmother and stepdaughter changed over the years and as she was the youngest of three children, unmarried and living closest to home, the responsibility fell to Judith to look after Angela following Ike's death, to assist in helping her find new homes, and to settle her estate after she died. She told me that Angela had always been besotted, head

over heels in love with Ike and his death came as a massive blow, indeed it was a very difficult time for everyone when he died. Angela was bereft and in a very bad way and appeared to be on the verge of a complete breakdown. Housekeeping had not been her strong point and the state of the home, already cluttered, untidy, in need of a good clean and packed high with books, worsened. Judith, as much for the memory and the love of her late father, did her best to console her stepmother and cope with the state of the house, but it was difficult. She did it 'with a good grace' though they 'didn't really have any empathy' in the hope that Angela was unaware of her true feelings.

It is easy to understand why housework was not

**1906-1979
an appreciation**

Produced to mark the opening of the Ike Gradwell
Community Suite, Link Centre, June 28th, 1985.

A lovely shared opening Tonight!
28 June 1985
COMMUNITY DEVELOPMENT

Angela Gradwell

The programme for the opening of the Ike Gradwell Suite at Swindon's Link Centre with Angela's comments and signed by her important to Angela. She had grown up in a home that employed servants to look after every day household needs and the mundane chores of housekeeping. There was so much more to occupy her busy life, her writing, her politics and her music, than the mere necessity of keeping a house clean. This contrasts sharply with the outward appearance of a woman who was, until her final years, always smartly dressed, well-organised and who appeared to be in total control. I am indebted to Judith Gradwell, not just for her memories of Angela, but for the generous loan of a number of family photographs. These, together with others people have given to me, perfectly illustrate the progression from a beautiful and self-possessed young woman to someone who was stylish and commanding in middle age and somewhat unorthodox in appearance in her final years.

Life for Angela after Ike's death must have seemed very empty. Others as well as Judith commented on how bereft and alone she appeared. Perhaps this encouraged her to go out more, campaigning for a variety of different causes, visiting folk clubs, festivals and political rallies throughout the region.

—9—
The Final Years

Many remember Angela busking on the streets of Swindon no matter how good or bad the weather might have been — a distinctive figure playing her concertina, to raise funds for the peace movement and in the mid-1980s for striking miners and their families. Angela understood the power of music, poetry and song. She knew that to sing with conviction could inspire and create comradeship and that the content of a song would take a message forward to convince others of a cause or belief and that throughout the history of folk song it had been used in response to one political situation or another. She was a regular visitor to Greenham Common to join those protesting against nuclear missiles at the base where she played her concertina and sang peace songs to raise the women's spirits. She still continued to drive her car well into her 80s though many said they were unwilling to accept a lift with her given that her driving could be erratic. Even before she gave up driving her friends were keen to offer her lifts to ensure her safety, and possibly their own!

Age was beginning to catch up with Angela and she moved into a flat at 23 David Stoddart Gardens, Omdurman Street in Swindon. Even so she continued to sell The Morning Star each day and continued to attend rallies and demonstrations; making sure that she visited the picket line of any local strikes every morning with copies of The Morning Star to keep them occupied as well as taking comforts of food and other necessary provisions. And she would play her concertina for the strikers, which someone less charitably suggested might, but for their resolve, have driven them back to work.

She had been greatly entertained by the irony in 1990 when the Thamesdown Council Offices from which Thatcher's hated Poll Tax, the Community Charge, was administered was named

Wat Tyler House, after the leader of the Peasants' Revolt in 1381 against the earlier Poll Tax. She was amused and annoyed that those less knowledgeable of their English history called the premises Rottweiler House!

Angela in her final years had no alternative due to failing health other than to move to an elderly persons' home in Swindon's Old Town. She was already suffering from vascular dementia though at first this was barely noticeable except to those who knew her well. She was also physically very healthy and outwardly appeared extremely robust.

The first residential home proved unsuitable, as the staff had no experience of looking after someone quite like Angela. They were accustomed to caring for residents who were physically or mentally more dependent and who rarely went out on their own or with others. Whereas Angela expected to go out for walks on her own, have meals as and when she wanted, and be taken to folk clubs, music sessions and other events by friends without telling the staff where she was going or when she would return. The staff were extremely good to her but it must have been very testing for those who had a duty of care and were responsible for her well being. After a short stay she investigated alternatives and moved to another more flexible residential home at Westlecott Manor on the edge of Old Town to enjoy her final years where the staff 'were happy to accept her foibles and eccentricities' and allow her the necessary amount of freedom to come and go as she pleased. It was from here that she was taken into hospital for a while when she required nursing care but she returned to the home where she died in August 1994 at the age of 88. Judith had been at her bedside during the day and left in the early evening. Later in the night she received a call to say that Angela had died. Her funeral took place at Kingsdown Crematorium in Swindon, as had her beloved Ike's some 15 years earlier. There is a commemorative bench close to the bandstand in Swindon's beautiful Town Gardens and a simple plaque that reads 'Angela Gradwell 1905 – 1994 who dedicated her life to international peace and solidarity. From Swindon Communists and Friends'. A few years later another commemorative plaque was installed next to Angela's. It reads, 'Les Thompson 1923 – 2010 Swindon AEU

District Secretary, a 'Jarrow lad' and lifelong socialist from Swindon Communists and friends'. No doubt Angela would have been proud to share the bench with such an illustrious and well-respected trade unionist, communist and anti-fascist.

Although ill health had dominated her final years she remained active in politics, stayed true to the Communist Party and labour movement, the peace movement and folk music until the end.

I attended a memorial event to celebrate her life in the Gradwell Suite at Swindon's Link Centre in November 1994 and wrote a short obituary of her in my column, under the name of Rosie Upton, in The Bath Chronicle. It was coincidental that she shared the page with a preview about Scottish folk singer Dick Gaughan whose revolutionary spirit she admired and, like Angela, had been active in supporting the strikers and their families during the Miners Strike of 1984 – 85.

Whatever views people may have about Marxist theory, communist ideology, the successes or the failures and disappointments that history has shown us in their implementation, especially during Stalin's regime, Angela must be admired for her unswerving devotion to the cause. She will be remembered as an inspirational character, a courageous woman, with boundless energy and vitality who had never waivered in her belief that a fairer and more equal society was achievable in which everyone had the opportunity to live a happy and fulfilled life; a peaceful society in which wealth was more evenly distributed; where no one need go hungry and where art and music were not merely the prerogative of the wealthy but accessible to all. She had worked ceaselessly throughout a long and eventful life towards this goal.

The commemorative bench in Swindon Town Gardens with a plaque saying: Angela Gradwell, 1906-1994, who dedicated her life to international peace and socialism. From Swindon Communists and friends

Angela Remembered

–10–
Memories of Folk Song and Revolution

I spoke to many people who had fond memories of Angela during the course of my research and I heard some wonderful stories. Though many commented on her 'infernal love of the concertina' they all said how much they loved and respected her even though her personality was flawed and enigmatic. She wasn't a bad concertina player, she had played in concertina orchestras both in Bristol and London and was used to accompanying herself and others, but her otherwise keen perception appeared to fail her when it came to knowing when to stop playing. Many remember her at Sidmouth International Folk Festival held annually at the beginning of August. She would sit on the low wall between the promenade and the road in the sunshine playing for hours, sometimes alone and more often with others, and regularly drew a crowd of appreciative holiday-makers and passers-by.

Angela on a Bath Hat and Feather 'folk cruise': Picture by Jan Holt

Olga Shotton told me that Angela was very knowledgeable about English folk song and especially proud of her Anglo concertina because it had once belonged to William Kimber, a dancer and concertina player to Heddington Quarry Morrismen and friend of English folksong collector Cecil Sharp.

Jan Holt, now in her 80s, who lives near Bath, was another of her many friends and she gave me a number of photos and greetings cards which included various quotations from great writers and thinkers, some useful proverbs, as well as Angela's own thoughts. Jan gave them to me for publication rather than be "kept by an ancient who treasured these quotes of Angela's". In one photograph Angela is on a narrowboat on the Kennet and Avon Canal near Bath, her jacket, as always, emblazoned with badges. It was a 'folk cruise' organised by the Hat and Feather Folk Club in Bath and as ever Angela was there playing her concertina. In another she is talking to a young Martin Carthy in Swindon Folk Singers Club run by stalwarts of the communist party and trade union movement Ted and Ivy Poole. Jan told me that after the war, when Churchill was 'helping' the royalists in Greece, Angela was given the task of taking cash to the patriots in the north of the country. She knew no Greek but in typical heroic style off she went with the money stashed inside her concertina. On another occasion Angela visited Jan in a village near Bath, owned by the Duchy of Cornwall, and sat in the dusty square playing her concertina. Children gathered and just as she had done in Greece all those years before Angela drew a hammer and sickle in the dust and told her story of the Greek Patriots. Jan remembered Angela's terrible driving – 'the offer of a lift in a car with Angela was to be avoided'!

I am indebted to Ted and Ivy Poole for all their help in piecing together Angela's story during the Swindon years. Ted remembers her as 'a hard taskmaster' and 'always determined in whatever she did'. He remembers receiving 'long missives from her on a variety of different subjects. Her knowledge of politics and traditional music was extensive but the trouble with Angela was that she didn't always know when to stop. She would come to the Folk Singers Club and have a song in her mind and be determined to sing it no matter what, how long or how out of keeping. She had her own way of doing things!' Ted remembers Ike

Angela with Martin Carthy at Swindon Folk Singers Club: Picture by Jan Holt.

Angela with Bob Cretchley, Ivy Poole and a group of Welsh Miners during the Miners Strike: Picture by the Swindon Advertiser

describing her as 'an original thinker'. They told me a story they had heard of a group of local workers during the Miner's Strike 'liberating' some food, quite large quantities in fact, held in a government storage depot on the Marlborough Downs and that Angela 'was prone to assist' in these clandestine operations. She may have had a legal training but it seems she was not afraid to break the law if the need, or greater good, warranted such direct action! The mark of a true revolutionary spirit perhaps?

Ted and Ivy remembered Irish singer Jim Coughlan telling them how he would often find Angela appearing as if from nowhere by the back door of his house playing her concertina, having walked from the Elderly Person's Home. He would make her a cup of tea and then make sure she was returned home safely. Ted and Ivy saw Angela on her last days in hospital. Though she was often confused she was still able to talk and hold a conversation. The last time they saw her was just before going away on holiday, probably to Sidmouth and Dartmoor Folk Festivals, and by the time they returned Angela was dead.

Although everyone loved and respected Angela there is no denying that Angela's choice of songs could be challenging and her concertina playing occasionally annoying, especially if prolonged, though there was also a hint of defiance in the way she played which undoubtedly reflected the strength of her personality. It is this determination that doubtless contributed to her achieving so much and leading such an energetic life almost until the end. Bob Cretchley, a Trade Unionist from Swindon and active member of Swindon Trades Council, remembers Angela from various marches and rallies. 'She would get on the bus with a stock of songs and attempt to encourage community singing on the way to each and every demonstration by playing her concertina. This had varying results and inevitably some unfortunate person would be sitting next to her. The younger people on the bus were always acutely embarrassed by these attempts at community singing. But worse was to come on the return journey when she would move to the front and insist on playing everyone off the coach as they arrived at their drop-off point. It was not unknown for people to avoid this embarrassment by staying on the bus until it reached its final destination. She always held a stock of leaflets which she would insist on handing out, more often than not to the converted!'

Bob also gave me a splendid photograph of himself, Ivy Poole and Angela with four miners in Swindon town centre during the Miner's Strike of 1984/5 collecting money. It was something Angela did whenever she was able and always wore a miner's helmet. Ivy Poole remembered Angela 'borrowing' a Tesco's shopping trolley that she kept in her house filled with all the banners, placards and leaflets. She would wheel it down to the centre of town every week, Fridays and Saturdays, when they were collecting. Angela would stay there all day and play her concertina most of the time 'whether or not people wanted to hear from her'. People just accepted it. Ivy remembers people would bring baskets of food as well as money to be taken back to Wales for the miners and their families. They raised many hundreds of thousand pounds. Ivy also has fond memories of Communist Party Bazaars held twice yearly at its own premises at Edith Stevens House, 77/78 Bridge Street to raise funds for the Morning Star and Angela would 'entertain' all day with her concertina. Angela had suggested the renaming of the property Edith Stevens House in 1970 when the party moved from its original premises previously called Edith Stevens House at 1 Bridge Street.

Edith Stevens who died in 1970 at the age of 86 was one of the founder members of the Swindon Branch of the Communist Party of Great Britain and remained politically active in Swindon well into her eighties. The daughter of a railway worker she went on to become a teacher and fighter for women's rights. She had been a dear friend of Ike and Angela. One of Edith's relatives told me that Angela had planned to write a brief biography of Edith and had collated notes to speak about her on local radio in 1984. This had apparently included one verse of a song about Edith. Unfortunately, despite a search through Angela's papers I was unable to trace the song, neither did Ted or Ivy Poole have any recollection of it.

Susan Camburn of Swindon Communist Party gave me a number of items that had been given to her by Angela. These included several pages from a diary kept whilst she travelled in the Soviet Union with Ike in 1962. One of the most impressive official visits on that trip had been to the Volga Hydroelectric Station. Afterwards they went for a swim in the river 'whilst Volga boatmen' steered vast rafts of felled timber past them. Angela comments that the river water was yellow and 'tasted of thick soup'! Susan also gave me a commemorative leaflet to Ike Gradwell prepared by Thamesdown Borough Council for the opening of the Gradwell Suite at Swindon's Link Centre on 28 June 1985. The leaflet is signed by Angela with the comment 'a lovely shared opening tonight!'. Susan recollects that Angela had never been particularly house-proud, surrounded by so many books and papers, and that it was becoming increasingly difficult for her to keep her home clean and tidy as she got older. However, once she was installed in the elderly person's home 'she would be out of the door, often first thing in the morning after breakfast, for a walk along the old canal or through the park. Despite infirmity she would walk miles and just keep going until she was too tired to continue, at which point she would flag down any car and ask bewildered strangers to give her a lift home'. Either too polite to turn her down, or worried about her health, the request worked without fail! Many of her old friends and her stepdaughter said they were concerned for her safety due to these habitual wanderings but the only alternative would have been to keep her locked in a home – and that would not have suited Angela!

As a member of the English Folk Song and Dance Society she was a regular visitor to folk song and dance events at Halsway Manor in Somerset. Chris Legge a fellow musician and member of Bristol's Folk Tradition remembers her sitting at the bar singing and playing her concertina. Even when living away from Bristol she continued to be a regular visitor to Bristol's Folk Tradition that had, by then, moved to a new home at The Nova Scotia in Hotwells. She rarely missed The Singer's Club in Swindon on Friday evenings, founded in 1960 by fellow communists Ted and Ivy Poole. She was a member for more than 30 years until her death. She was also a member of the International Concertina Association and during her years in London I was told she played with a concertina orchestra that regularly used to broadcast and give concerts.

Brian Hankins had taken a job as an English teacher at the newly established Hreod Burna Comprehensive Upper School in Swindon in 1967. He was 30 years old at the time and became a regular at the folk club in Swindon where he met Angela. He said 'I soon became aware of an elderly (to me then) dignified-looking lady, who played the concertina incredibly slowly to accompany her renderings of interminably long, meandering ballads. Within a few weeks, I came to dread these performances and to use them, if I spotted them early enough not to cause offence, as an opportunity for a toilet break! I knew nothing of her history and only a little more of folk ballads. I left Swindon at the end of 1971, but was able to make occasional return visits from 1981 onwards. By then, two things had changed. Angela – supported by a club with a carefully supportive attitude to players and singers striving for competence – had become a performer worth listening to. Also, I had learned to appreciate traditional English ballads. I gradually discovered some of her history (probably from Ted Poole) but, sadly for me, I moved from feelings of impatience to feelings of awe, neither of which is conducive to friendly, relaxed conversation.'

Some have questioned, in the light of what history has revealed about Stalin and the communist state, why she remained

steadfast to her beliefs. Perhaps
for Angela communism was the
only viable alternative to fascism.
The propaganda machinery
during her visits to the Soviet
block would have been in full
force and there is no doubt that
she had been impressed by what
she saw. Official visitors would
have been carefully monitored
throughout their stay and only
shown the successes such as the
economic benefits of
industrialisation and increased
power output. The truth about
the purges and the harmful
impact of collectivisation of
agriculture leading to mass
starvation were only fully
revealed later after the
dissolution of the USSR. Stalin

*Angela at a Workers' Music
Association Summer School at Wortley
Hall near Sheffield in 1987*

was a tyrant and dictator whose totalitarian regime tainted world
opinions of the communist state. The Berlin Wall fell in 1989 just
five years before her death and Soviet President Mikhail
Gorbachev resigned at the end of 1991 ending the Cold War less
than three years before she died, by which time she was already
suffering some memory loss. I think Angela had a utopian view
of a classless society where there is greater equality for all. It is a
dream that most regard as unrealistic and unlikely to be achieved
but something to which many would aspire. Indeed, there are
some today who continue to support Marxist theory and believe
that his vision is achievable. I am of the opinion that Angela was
far too intelligent and questioning to have easily been taken in by
any misinformation and too strong-minded to have been
indoctrinated but she was an idealist with a passionate, if
somewhat romantic belief in a utopian future. We all have our
beliefs and no matter how irrational a view may seem to others,
we continue to hold onto it with an obstinate conviction that it is

true. There is no evidence to suggest that Angela supported Stalin once the facts emerged but she did believe that the pursuit of Marxism would lead to a better world.

Many of those I talked to remember Angela as energetic, capable, confident, uncompromising and strong-willed with a resolute determination that she carried with her to the end. Something that socialist, political activist, musician and writer Ken Keable perfectly sums up from meeting Angela when they both attended the Workers' Music Association Summer School in 1987. It was held, as usual, at Wortley Hall (known as "the workers' stately home") in Yorkshire. He already knew of her, as a fellow communist, by reputation through the Morning Star. He remembers her singing folk and political songs, accompanying herself on the concertina. He said 'She was a strong personality and not a very disciplined person as I remember, sometimes trying something out on her concertina when she should have been listening to a tutor. Sharing her political and musical interests, I admired her as a woman who was strong-willed and politically committed and who remained active despite being 80 or 81 years of age. This story coincides with comments received from two others who asked not to be quoted by name. A fellow concertina player praised Angela's many qualities but commented 'such a pity about her concertina playing, she never knew when to stop!' Another said 'it was unfortunate that often when I sang and she was seated close by she would insist on playing her concertina, frequently in a different key and more often than not a completely different tune'. Many will acknowledge that Angela's ability as a singer and folk musician was not equal to her enthusiasm. Though having only heard her performing in later life it is impossible to judge whether this was always the case. Perhaps she was naïve in not realising that the reaction to her performances was not always favourable, or perhaps she just got on with the job in hand and didn't notice.

Bob Naylor, a photojournalist and NUJ member, captured the wonderful image used on the book cover showing Angela, playing her concertina at the gates of Greenham Common with decorated paper cut-out doves seeming to spring from within her. Bob remembers her from her time in Swindon. He said, "It might seem harsh in retrospect but we all loved her though sometimes she appeared a bit like someone from the middle class teaching the working class about their own culture".

I don't see these comments as especially cruel or controversial. Angela was of a certain class and grew up in an age where class still counted yet she had an empathy with ordinary working people and understood their struggles. She was not especially wealthy and lived frugally for the latter part of her life and to some extent their struggles had become her own. It is a criticism that has been levelled at many philanthropists, educators and folk song collectors such as Cecil Sharp. They regarded themselves as progressive and able to educate and improve those they regarded as coming from the 'underclass' and largely illiterate. Indeed, fellow folksong scholar and Marxist AL Lloyd was hugely critical of Sharp's attitude to those ordinary singers, whilst still recognising his great achievement in collecting songs that would otherwise have been lost. I don't believe Angela regarded herself as better than others, far from it, but I am equally certain that without such people many important social improvements would not have been achieved and the oral tradition of folk song would not have been preserved as a valuable historical record. Angela in her own way reminded us that there was a need for change in society and that there is much we can learn from history and one of the best ways of communication is through the powerful message of song.

During the 1970s and 80s, Chipping Sodbury Folk Club met every Saturday evening in a barnlike building to the rear of The George Hotel. Run by Malcolm Penny, a charismatic wildlife writer and filmmaker and the twins, Joc and Dill, it was one of the most popular folk clubs in the area and Angela was a regular visitor. Bristolian folk singer and songwriter Mike Scott reported that 'For a few years she was my preferred 'sit next to' person at Chipping Sodbury Folk Club, as she always had a few pertinent and positive comments to make during the evening. I well remember one particular occasion, when Great Britain was winning some prestigious medals at the Olympics, (the Seoul Olympics of 1988), and the hockey team had just won Gold, and were unavoidable in every element of the media, TV, radio, newspapers and integral to every conversation with casual acquaintances. I prefaced my song that evening with an undeniably boorish rant against the 'bloody hockey', Angela sat next to me apparently neither amused nor upset, but when the opportunity arose, she quietly whispered, 'Hockey is a very fine game you know, I played for England.' Now my memory might have inserted the word England, where some less impressive honour had been bestowed, like Wiltshire, or Swindon, but I do believe she played at a fairly elevated level, I don't want to be told it wasn't England!'

Mike and Maggie Starkey from Yate in South Gloucestershire also knew Angela well. Angela used to stay with a mutual friend Graham Bevan who ran the folk club in Chipping Sodbury after Malcolm left. It relocated to The Portcullis when The George closed. Angela continued to attend on most Saturday evenings when she was able. They remember her 'as a staunch feminist who knew all the political songs and their history, but she never talked down to anyone'. However, 'if someone sang something that she regarded as inappropriate she would counter it with a politically charged song and was never afraid to make a comment'. Mike and Maggie used to collect her on Sunday lunchtimes and drive her back to Swindon where they would all go to the regular Irish session and afterwards drive her home. Angela would thoroughly enjoy herself joining in and singing some of her favourite traditional songs including 'My Singing Bird' and 'The Cutty Wren' which some claim has its origins in the Peasants' Revolt.

Betty McDonald, a noted folk singer originally from Tyneside but who spent most of her life in South Gloucestershire where both she and her singing partner husband Norman worked at Oldbury Power Station, died in October 2014. I interviewed her when she was well into her 80s. She remembered Angela towards the end of her life and recollects how she was always desperate to escape with the slightest excuse from the home where she spent her final years. She had a number of friends, Betty and Norman included, who would act with others as her 'escape committee' to take her out for the evening, often driving many miles to Swindon and back.

Mick Ryan, a well known folksinger of Irish descent and composer of folk operas, lodged at Angela's house for a time. He became very fond of her and told me that he had never seen a house so packed with books. Ted Poole also remembered the books and said that the garage at the house she shared with Ike was 'full of books, a library in the back garden, filled from floor to ceiling'.

I was amused by a former member of the Communist Party and retired Regional Secretary of UNISON who when I asked if he remembered Angela referred to her as 'one scary woman'. Formidable, perhaps, but not in an intimidating way, though I must confess to being a little scared of her myself, if not in total awe. She had once upbraided me for being frivolous after I had sung a song she regarded as inappropriate and pandering to the male ego. I said that although it may have seemed playful, at least the woman in the song had defeated the man at his own game, but this was not sufficient and I received something of a lecture about women's rights. We also spoke of the negative manner in which women are portrayed in folk song and ballad. They come off particularly badly; nearly always the victim in a man's world, but regrettably that has been the reality for the greater part of history and remains so today in many parts of the world. We agreed that it is something we need to remember, to celebrate the lives of those women forgotten or undervalued by history and to educate those who know no different by singing these songs to give those women and others like them today a voice.

Her story is extraordinary but I have been intrigued wondering why Angela chose to start writing an autobiography. I doubt it was simply vanity, though anyone with the confidence to perform and speak in public must have the necessary ego, or even that she felt her life was more important than others. I think it more likely that she understood the significance of history and the importance of knowledge. I think Angela's story is important and lessons can be learnt about the importance of remaining true to your own beliefs and having the strength to stand up for yourself and for those who might not otherwise have a voice. History has been cruel to women. Written for the most part by men, the exploits of women have rarely been recorded with the same eagerness or veracity as our male counterparts. It was with this in mind that I started on my journey to discover more of the real Angela and record her history, however briefly. It is something I had felt for a very long time was well overdue.

I hope readers will have enjoyed reading Angela's story. I hope I've created a full and convincing a portrayal of the real person. I've included the memories of those who praised her as well as those who found some aspects of Angela's personality trying and her enthusiasm for the concertina more than a little irksome. I don't think these stories devalue her memory but contribute to a more rounded picture of a woman who had flaws, who could occasionally appear obsessive and domineering, but in her own way brought some pleasure into the lives of many. I hope it is a fair and convincing depiction of a woman with a strong and determined character who was loved and respected rather than simply an idealised portrait. There will undoubtedly have been omissions and I sense that more people will come forward with their own memories of her but too late for this publication.

–11–
Angela in print

There is a massive archive of material relating to Angela. It would be a huge task to read and chronicle everything, the sort of task that would not have daunted Angela, but which sadly I can't begin to contemplate! She was extremely well-read, an almost compulsive diarist and a writer who carefully recorded events in her own life and every detail of the subject she was researching and writing about. She kept a meticulous log of her sources and ensured that they were properly documented, indexed and maintained as a bibliography in all her books.

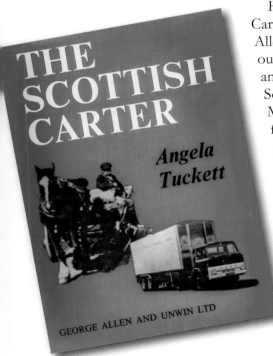

Her book The Scottish Carter published in 1967 by Allen and Unwin, and long out of print, is a fascinating and detailed history of The Scottish Horse and Motormen's Association from 1898 – 1964 when it merged with the T&GWU (now Unite). The sleeve note describes Angela and the book as follows:

'Angela Tuckett is an active trade unionist, and has practical knowledge of the trade union movement in the capacity of a qualified solicitor and

UP WITH ALL THAT'S DOWN!
A History of Swindon Trades Council
by
ANGELA TUCKETT

1891-1971

journalist. She explains the development of the men's outlook, from the relations which obtained between master and servant in the intolerable conditions of the horse-drawn era to the present-day crisis in collective bargaining.'

Her other two major works of non-fiction 'The Blacksmiths' History: What smithy workers gave trade unionism' published in 1974 by Lawrence and Wishart, and 'The Scottish Trades Union Congress: The First 80 Years 1897 – 1977' published in 1986 by Mainstream are equally detailed and essential reading for anyone interested in the history of trades unionism and the labour movement.

Angela wrote the definitive history of Swindon Trades Council 1891 – 1971, 'Up With All That's Down!' published in 1971 by The Quill Press. Although very detailed and perhaps not of the greatest interest other than to local historians and trade unionists it is a surprisingly good read. The acrid smell of engine oil, soot and poverty permeates the pages as Angela so precisely charts the working class struggle, the need to organise and the origins of the Swindon Labour Party. The battles with the powerful owners of the Great Western Railway, the General Strike of 1926 and the human stories of Alderman Reuben George whose slogan when he fought an election was 'Down with all that's up' and the self-taught poet, author and folk song collector Alfred Williams, known as the Hammerman Poet, who spent his working life operating a steam hammer in the railway works, can be found here.

Angela was immensely proud of her aunt Enid Stacy and her

achievements and legacy as a celebrated if unluckily short-lived feminist, socialist, trades unionist and campaigner for social reform. Towards the end of her life she began writing a biography of Enid but sadly this was never finished and the parts that remain are often confused and inconsistent. She did succeed in writing an article about Enid, who had moved with her husband Rev Percy Widdrington to Calderbrook, Lancashire and this was published in 1980 entitled 'Enid Stacy' and formed part of the North West Labour History Society Bulletin 7 1980 – 81.

The Blitz and the misery it caused horrified Angela but also inspired her to write poetry. 'Verses Against Fascism and War' is a collection of poems about the years of fascist dictatorships of the 1930s and 40s and ending with peace. The first written in 1934 and eventually published as a collection in December 1979.

A couple of good examples as an ending to this brief history of an exceptional life follow, together with a song she wrote, clearly about her relationship with her first husband. It is in the style of an English or Irish folksong but where a traditional song would have ended with the wronged young woman complaining bitterly about her fate or even killing herself, Angela's strength and determination is clearly shown in the ending… she left him!

Independent Lover

When I was young and fell in love
I'd fetch the stars to please him
But sun and moon were not enough
Nothing might ease him

He stole my heart and right good will
Ah these I'd not deny him
And bade me stand there constant till
The mood passed by him

And I should sing his praise the while
And never cease to tell him
That never a one lived in this isle
Who might excel him

So much in love I was inclined
In all things to obey him
But could not yield him up my mind
So could not stay him

He railed at me right bitterly
But still I would not grieve him
So nothing was there left for me
To do – but leave him

Second Front Eve

Each homely sound a greater meaning bears
A child's shrill cry at play cuts deep
Recalls those over there who weep
No sound but warns us a great moment nears

A rapid step at night along the street
Machinery thudding – traffic's roar
A sudden knocking at the door
The cockcrow, and the blacksmith's hammer beat

Familiar sounds a deeper meaning bear
We turn and stop to listen, still
For distant clash of steel on steel
The tide is making and the wind is fair

No homely sounds till they are home again
No summer joy in tree and flower
No common words can match this hour
No common words can match our fighting man

Life Sentence

You will not see this lovely spring
Nor watch the seagull's wheeling flight
For you no nesting birds will sing
To part still day from silent night

Long summer evenings pass you by
And autumn's never a harvest bring
Nor winter's pregnant pause will lie
So quietly encompassing

All season's past till death? Ah, No
Although fast held behind their bars
You live, you strike a hammer blow
With every heart-beat timed to ours

It's for their lifetime, not your own
That sentence runs; and there shall be
Another Bastille overthrown
And you, with all your kind, set free

Then we shall share a lovelier spring
And watch the gull's exultant flight
The larks released rise up and sing
As glorious day succeeds to night

Angela's Publications

Civil Liberty and the Industrial Worker. 1942, National Council for Civil Liberties

The Scottish Carter. 1967, Allen and Unwin

Up With All That's Down! 1971, The Quill Press

Yesterday, Today and Tomorrow. 1973

Verses against War and Fascism. (A collection of poetry written between 1935 and 1945) 1979.

The Blacksmiths' History: what smithy workers gave trade unionism. 1974, Lawrence and Wishart

Sing and Stay Human. 1977

The People's Theatre in Bristol 1930–45. Our History Pamphlet 72. 1979, Communist Party of GB

Enid Stacy. Bulletin 7. 1980–81 (pages 41–48), North West Labour History Society

Ike Gradwell 1906–1979, Man of the People; a memoir' published in 1980 by Angela

The Scottish Trades Union Congress: The First 80 Years 1897–1977. 1986, Mainstream

Angela recognised as one of Swindon's Greatest Headline Makers

On 24 June 2015 the Swindon Advertiser, on the 160th anniversary of the newspaper, published a souvenir supplement of Swindon's Greatest Headline Makers whose work or achievements had helped raise the standing of the town or had improved the lives of ordinary people.

Angela supporting striking miners
Picture by Swindon Advertiser

Angela appeared in the list as Angela Gradwell, the name by which she was known in the town. It is something of which she would undoubtedly have been proud and perhaps a little amused to appear in a list that included James Bond's creator, Ian Fleming and Miss Whiplash, but also poet and folk song collector Alfred Williams whose work she very much admired. Ted and Ivy Poole to whom this book is dedicated also appear in the list.

The Tuckett family lines

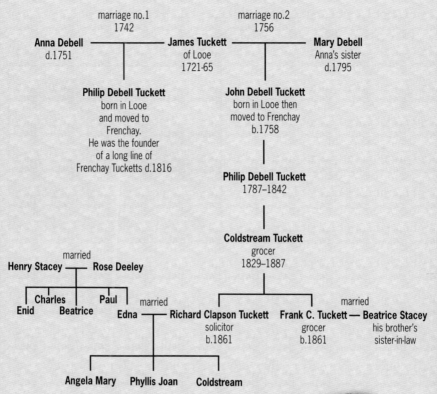

marriage no.1
1742

marriage no.2
1756

Anna Debell
d.1751

James Tuckett
of Looe
1721-65

Mary Debell
Anna's sister
d.1795

Philip Debell Tuckett
born in Looe
and moved to
Frenchay.
He was the founder
of a long line of
Frenchay Tucketts d.1816

John Debell Tuckett
born in Looe then
moved to Frenchay
b.1758

Philip Debell Tuckett
1787–1842

Coldstream Tuckett
grocer
1829–1887

married

Henry Stacey ——— **Rose Deeley**

Charles | **Paul**
Enid | **Beatrice**

married

Edna ——— **Richard Clapson Tuckett**
solicitor
b.1861

Frank C. Tuckett — **Beatrice Stacey**
grocer
b.1861

married

his brother's
sister-in-law

Angela Mary **Phyllis Joan** **Coldstream**

The Tucketts, who moved to the Bristol area from Cornwall in the 18th century, were prominent merchants and traders.

Well respected as Quakers and philanthropists, they contributed much to the life and prosperity of the city.

Their descendants like Angela inherited much of their beliefs in equality and peace as well as a spirit of defiance and unconventionality.

Acknowledgements

Sources:

Individuals and others to whom I am indebted for their assistance, old photographs and memories of Angela:

Individuals

Bob Blake, Susan Camburn, Nigel Costley, SW Regional Secretary TUC, Bob Cretchley, Professor John Foster, Ian Freke, Curator of Frenchay Museum, Judith Gradwell, Brian Hankins, Linda Hares,. Di Harris, Jan Holt, Ken Keable, Chris Legge, Betty McDonald, Bob Naylor, Ted and Ivy Poole, Mick Ryan, Olga Shotton, Mike and Maggie Starkey.

Together with a number of others who have asked not be named.

Organisations and others

Bristol Central Reference Library, Bristol Law Society, Bristol Museum and Art Gallery, Bristol Records Office, Bristol Savages, British Library, Marx Memorial Library, Oxford Dictionary of National Biography, South West TUC, The Tuckett Society and Frenchay Museum, Working Class Movement Library (Salford) and Warwick University Modern Records Centre.

Thanks

Dreweatts and Bloomsbury Auctions for permission to use a photograph of a provisions tin.

Angela's unpublished and incomplete autobiography kindly loaned by Professor John Foster and without which my research would have been far more difficult.

Special thanks to Liz Payne-Ahmadi for making contact on my behalf with Professor John Foster to whom I am indebted for his generous loan of Angela's papers.

Ted and Ivy Poole deserve a special mention for their help in piecing together the Swindon years and so much more.

Angela's stepdaughter Judith Gradwell for her help, good humour and clarification as well as for the generous loan and permission to use various papers and old family photographs.

Bernard Barry's 'Angela Tuckett, 1906-1994, her story' at the Working Class Movement Library was an essential starting point in tracing her story. Also thanks to the staff, in particular Lynette, at Working Class Movement Library for making me feel at home with mugs of tea and bringing seemingly endless boxes of Angela's papers from storage in their cellar, and for contacting Judith Gradwell, Angela's stepdaughter on my behalf.

Thanks to Nigel Costley, Secretary of SW TUC for his help and encouragement.

A special thanks to Bob Naylor and Di Harris of WaterMarx for all their hard work and dedication in designing, editing, setting and publishing this book.

Sponsors

Without their financial support, this publication would not have been possible:

Thompsons Solicitors, Simpson Millar Solicitors, Musicians' Union, National Union of Journalists (Bristol and Swindon Branches), UNISON, Unite the Union, GMB, NASUWT, South West TUC, WaterMarx Publishers, White Horse Wiltshire Trades Council and a number of anonymous donors.

List of Illustrations